A PRACTICAL GUIDE

OUTDOOR LEARNING

KEVIN JACKSON

A JOHN CATT PUBLICATION

First published 2015
by John Catt Educational Ltd,
12 Deben Mill Business Centre, Old Maltings Approach,
Melton, Woodbridge IP12 1BL
Tel: +44 (0) 1394 389850
Fax: +44 (0) 1394 386893
Email: enquiries@johncatt.com
Website: www.johncatt.com

ISBN: 978 1 909717 62 6

Set and designed by Theoria Design Ltd
www.theoriadesign.com

Printed and bound in Great Britain
by Charlesworth Press

Contents

Preface

by Richard Howard
Chair, National Education Trust

Even 40 years on, when I meet former pupils in the street, they always mention one thing about their schooldays – the residential trip that they went on. Perhaps it was to Exmoor, the Isle of Wight, North Norfolk, or the Peak District. Something about those week-long trips has remained with them over the years. That 'something' is usually about learning new skills, working together, leaving home for the first time, or just the pure enjoyment and excitement of experiencing a new environment.

In this informative, practical and authoritative Guide, Kevin Jackson sets out the rationale and the methodology for undertaking outdoor and adventurous learning. It inspires enthusiasm for real learning and growing. It provides opportunities for children, young people and their teachers to seek experiences that will become memorable and develop life-long interests.

I really hope that the book will inspire even more schools to enjoy the challenges and pleasures from spending time away from the classroom and, by so doing, to learn even more.

"Twenty years from now, you will be more disappointed by the things you didn't do than those you did. So throw off the bowlines. Sail away from safe harbor. Catch the wind in your sails. Explore. Dream. Discover."

Mark Twain

My background

For me it started a long time ago in 1980 and within a couple of years of starting my teaching career I realised I was spending more time in a tent than in the classroom. Fortunately, I had a Head who took the brave step of creating a Head of Outdoor Education post within the school, delivering programmes to a 1200 pupil comprehensive in Birmingham. This was a real adventure and charted the unknown, but a great opportunity to explore and link learning outside with learning inside, working with and alongside innovative and inspirational figures within the outdoor world. Since then various moves have led to my current post as Service Lead for Oxfordshire Outdoors.

The outcomes of many and varied experiences along the way, at personal and professional levels, have formed a firm conviction that participation in well thought out and properly constructed adventure based learning really does have a significant impact on personal development, with real and transferable benefits of increased self-confidence; positive social awareness and interaction.

The challenge lies in convincing parents, teachers, school leaders, politicians *et al* that the impact is real, beneficial and is worthwhile investing resources in.

Context

The aim of this book is to join the dots and create a picture, bringing together practical examples; sources of advice; quality assurance; relevance and rationale into a single source reference document. In doing so hopefully it will both encourage and challenge current and prospective visit leaders to think about how they can widen opportunities and enable access to high quality learning experiences, resulting in more children and young people experiencing the very considerable and real benefits adventurous outdoor learning in a residential setting offers.

I know of many committed teachers who organise and deliver high quality courses for their groups and no doubt this will be the same across the country. Equally there are many teachers unsure of what high quality looks like; or are simply unsure of how to go about organising such courses. The aim of this guide is to celebrate the former and help inspire the latter.

Asking outdoor professionals and teachers leading residential courses how they would describe an adventure based residential experience in a single word, the most common responses were:

Inspirational, adventurous, motivating, challenging, fun, real, lifelong, satisfying, developmental

These could just as easily be descriptors for a quality classroom based curriculum.

With the rapidly changing face of education and the prediction that current learners will face a diverse range of careers and need to be equipped for this, the benefits and contribution of a carefully constructed outdoor learning programme should not be underestimated.

So let's start by looking at the rationale for **why** we should include adventure based learning in our curriculum.

Making the case –
school-based outdoor learning

"For some children a week's residential experience is worth more than a term of school. We know we want it for our own children - we need to make sure other people's children experience it too."

Sir Tim Brighouse,
former London Schools Commissioner

The key question for teachers and leaders is how to identify high quality experiences and to integrate the value and benefits into the school ethos and curriculum, so that it becomes an integral feature, a pupil expectation and not an extra.

Question: At what age should schools offer an adventure based residential experience?

I was recently discussing this with a teacher who had just organised the first school residential, camping on the school site, for the Foundation phase at his school. What an adventure (for staff and children alike) and what a start to school life. This experience, as with Forest School[1] programmes, is fast becoming the norm. It allows schools to become more expansive in how and where they plan residential experiences as the children move through.

Within our Oxfordshire Outdoors centres we are seeing such 'experienced' Yr 6 pupils, which means we can raise the bar and offer progressive and differentiated levels of challenge in our programmes. Achieving these standards is important, and places a challenge into the secondary sector.

Question: What happens beyond the Primary phase?

Does the secondary sector proactively identify existing skills and experiences and seek to develop these further? Experience would suggest that this is not consistently embedded nor recognised as having the potential for enhancing learning. More worryingly, some simply choose not to plan their school programmes around pupil skills which then becomes an opportunity lost, with a potential consequence of demotivation.

The introduction of the revised 2014 National Curriculum provides opportunities for schools in England to broaden their delivery of Outdoor Learning, but how many schools are? More importantly, how many are aware of the potential that adventure based learning holds for their pupils and for their school?

A significant opening for teachers in English schools lies in the PE curriculum[2], which provides the detail for the inclusion of Outdoor and Adventurous Activities across KS 2-4. This is an excellent opportunity, especially with the announcement of an additional £450 million over 3 years through to 2016[3] to support and enhance PE in primary schools. So, what might this look like if it were linked, say to PSHE?

An example of curriculum linkage

Primary PE	PSHE - Health and Wellbeing Key Stages 1 and 2, pupils should be taught:
• are physically active for sustained periods of time • engage in competitive sports and activities • lead healthy, active lives. • KS2 – take part in outdoor and adventurous activity challenges both individually and within a team	• what is meant by a healthy lifestyle • how to maintain physical, mental and emotional health and wellbeing • how to manage risks to physical and emotional health and wellbeing • ways of keeping physically and emotionally safe • about managing change, including puberty, transition and loss • how to make informed choices about health and wellbeing and to recognise sources of help with this • how to respond in an emergency • to identify different influences on health and wellbeing

As a starter this provides a sound framework for an adventure based course, now add into this the relevance of other curriculum links and the framework expands. PSHE is used in this example as currently it is being pushed hard for wider recognition.

An adventure based residential course, if it is of high quality, must make the connections between the people; the learning; the venue; the activities and the environments in which they take place.

Thinking in terms of real, natural environments and thinking more laterally in terms of what can be built into an adventure learning programme, I would argue that real learning is achieved in real environments, not the imagined, sanitised virtual world.

To support this, a key action is to raise teacher confidence and awareness so that recognition and understanding necessary to organise and/or commission some or all of their outdoor learning programmes is in place. Ensuring high quality experiences, delivering teacher and group outcomes, is key. Teachers will need to know how and where to access information and how to determine quality provision. Examples of how this might happen are provided later.

Evidence trails

Robin Hammerton, HMI[4], included in a presentation to the 2011 Council for Learning Outside the Classroom (CLOtC) Conference confirmed memorable activities led to *memorable learning and the place where activities happened often added to their value.* Think back to your own school time, what burning memories do you have? What's the betting a significant number of responses would be of some form of residential visit?

Further the Ofsted view of the value of Learning Outside the Classroom (LOtC) was that *it contributed significantly to 'staying safe' and LOtC had positive benefits for all groups of young people, including those underachieving or not sufficiently motivated by mainstream provision* and having spent a career working across the broad spectrum of educational provision, this certainly holds resonance.

This position still holds, which effectively means that Ofsted recognition of LOtC continues. For example, in 2012 it reported on Neston High School[5]:

Neston High School secures high attainment and levels of progress through a well-integrated curriculum with a broad programme of learning outside the classroom (LOTC). This includes many residential visits, day trips and activities in the local environment. A 'can do' culture, more than any of the formal systems, adds the most value to enabling students to achieve well and thrive.

And in its 2013 report on Lavington Park Federation Ofsted[6] stated:

An example of a journey of discovery at two small federated schools in West Sussex as they utilise the rich resource of the outdoor environment to improve provision and engagement with pupils and learning. It illustrates the journey towards excellence and focuses on strategies to use the local environment to improve not only geography but also other subjects as part of an integrated approach to the curriculum.

So, if we have Ofsted endorsement of outdoor learning; the revised curriculum makes provision within PE and has funding allocated, what else is required to create acceptance of adventurous learning in schools?

Many schools will cite funding as being a significant barrier, but again this need not be so. Neston High proves the point and underlines that using Pupil Premium is ok.

Again Ofsted[7] evidence supports the case, in assessing the use and effectiveness of the Pupil Premium spend, it reported a *third of schools had used Pupil Premium funding to subsidise or pay for educational trips and residential visits and that schools also commonly said that they used the Pupil Premium to provide a wider range of curriculum opportunities and/ or to ensure that money did not become a barrier to equality of access to an enhanced curriculum.*

This provides schools with an increased confidence that it is ok to use the funding to support off site learning programmes. Further still Ofsted[8], in its update on the Pupil Premium July 2014, refers to the use of the premium to support educational visits, stating:

> The funding is also commonly used to enable eligible pupils to participate fully in after-school clubs and activities and to provide financial support for educational visits. In secondary schools, the funding is often used to provide after-school, weekend and holiday sessions.

Securing the evidence

A high quality adventurous residential experience will provide the opportunity to capture evidence of targeted interventions and it is relatively easy to achieve. How? One way is to use combinations of photos, film and live interviews, both at the time and later once back in the classroom.

Imagine this scene, the teacher records:

At the top of the cliff, a group of children sat gazing at the waves approaching the base of the climbs where, during the last few hours, they spent their day climbing and abseiling and held safety ropes for each other. The teacher guides them through a review of their day, enabling discussion around fears; anxieties; safety; successes; how this might guide future thinking … inspirational and powerful learning?

Now imagine this scene:

A few weeks/months later the teacher replays the conversations and links the learning then to a current classroom based challenge the students are facing ... recalling the 'I can' factor that led to the initial success. Equally powerful learning?

We will come back to this again.

If we have the potential to create such powerful and lasting learning, why is it that it is not universally recognised? Can we, should we, expect Government to provide the lead?

Character, resilience and grit...

'whatever qualifications you might have, where you are on the character scale will have a big impact on what you can achieve in life.'

Character and Resilience Manifesto[9]

In January 2014, an all-parliamentary group on social mobility produced a Character and Resilience Manifesto[10] (from which the recent Character Awards emerged) in which it looked at

how character traits and resilience are directly linked to being able to do well both at school and in the workplace... how working with young people with low self-esteem on building resilience to setbacks and developing an increased sense of control over their lives had led to improved literacy and numeracy results ...

Government has now picked up the baton.

In January 2015 Nicky Morgan, Secretary of State for Education[11] decided that character education was important enough to warrant a new initiative, with schools being able to access grant funding to support delivery. Programmes should *'develop character traits, attributes and behaviours that underpin success in school and work.'*

In May 2015 Nicky Morgan built on this further, announcing funding for rugby coaches[12] to build character and resilience in pupils[13] which *'includes a £5 million pledge to ensure that more pupils leave school prepared for the challenges of life in modern Britain, including £4 million to reward and spread the character work of school and charities, and £1 million to research the most effective approaches. An additional £5 million has also been awarded to life-changing projects run by former armed services personnel.'*

Following the May 2015 election, Children and Families Minister Edward Timpson has new responsibilities, including 'character and resilience', bullying, cadets and military ethos and PSHE.

Outside of Government there has also been some action. In June 2015 DEMOS published its own research Character Nation[14] in which it calls for *'the new government should embed the development of character throughout the institutions of formal and non-formal education across England.'*

The Institute for Health Promotion and Education (IHPE) has produced its own Safety Manifesto[15] in which it calls on Government to enable children and young people to learn by experiencing risk.

In doing so it specifically states that *through outdoor and adventurous activities at day and residential centres, children and young people should be given opportunities to engage in controlled activities which have elements of risk to identify and manage. Such activities necessarily include an opportunity for benefit or gain, a risk of loss or harm, and progression in the extent of challenge.*

Taking all this into account, let's go back to our climbing group. The teacher and Centre tutor are engaged in a review session with the group.

One student talks about how they stuck at it to ensure they reached the top of the climb; another about why it's important not to give up when things don't work out; another about how she developed a trust in her friends as they were holding her ropes; another about how peer support drove her on; another the need to act safely in this type of terrain ... as a group they understood the need for working together and for taking responsibility for their own actions ... and by the way this is for real and I witnessed such a session recently.

Nicky Morgan's criteria of *perseverance, resilience and grit; motivation, drive and ambition; confidence; tolerance and respect* are now very apt descriptors for this experience, providing the relevance and context for such traits to be developed and built on.

There exists a golden opportunity to put in place accessible programmes that have real impact, but to do so requires some joined up thinking and wider engagement. It is both perplexing and frustrating that DfE does not appear willing to acknowledge or engage with those delivering adventure based learning or even to recognise the benefits of this work. Yet the National Citizen Service[16], whose origins lie with the Prime Minister, is totally reliant on adventure based providers to deliver its residential component.

This concept of 'character and resilience' is not new and we should not blindly accept that it is, let alone accept it is the 'brainchild' of Government. The outdoor sector has been successfully delivering this for a very long time, those who focus on high quality delivery will know exactly what I mean, as will those teachers who continue to use high quality experiences to develop their pupils.

By not including adventure based learning in the 'character' mix the DfE excludes a lead sector well versed in delivering 'character' education. Maybe it needs a Minister to spend some time in a Centre to see what really happens, the offer is there.

Fortunately, this does not prevent schools from creating opportunities to further enrich and enhance personal development through participation in adventure based learning and it would appear that this is slowly but surely a growing trend.

It is no coincidence that within Oxfordshire Outdoors we have seen a shift in KS2 bookings, with schools saying they prefer the autumn term so they can spend the rest of the year building on the successes they achieve in their courses, and this happened long before this latest Govt initiative.

Other sources

There are wider sources of evidence to substantiate the value of adventure based residential learning, all of which contribute to making the case.

The Outward Bound Trust, in its Social Impact Report 2014[17], demonstrates its courses can have a *positive and sustained effect on young people's attitudes, skills and behaviour, helping them to become more effective individuals who are able to thrive throughout their education and employment*

The Paul Hamlyn Foundation commissioned its Learning Away Brilliant Residentials[18] research programme to assess the impact and value of a residential experience. Working closely with over 60 primary, secondary and special schools in 13 partnerships across the UK, Learning Away aims to enhance young people's learning, achievement and wellbeing by developing, piloting and evaluating the impact of residential experiences as an integral part of the curriculum.

In May 2015 York Consulting[19] published its final report on the programme, *with clearly stated benefits including residentials can significantly improve students' resilience, self-confidence, and sense of wellbeing together with residentials can significantly improve students' engagement with their learning, leading to improved school attendance and behaviour.*

Further quotes to help set the scene:

> *"We've not excluded anyone from the first year so far this year. The only difference is that we're now running transition residentials with our partner primary schools."*
>
> Secondary Head teacher, Calderglen High School

"Whilst you're there you don't have a mum to tell you what time to go to bed, get off the X-box, go and do your homework... It's more like taking control of your thing and making sure that you are on time, making sure that you've got to take control of your own situations."

Secondary student focus group

"We have seen a real benefit to holding residentials at different times of the year and the positive impact that this has had on staff/pupil relations. Similarly, we have seen a marked impact on pupil engagement and motivation."

Learning Away Coordinator, Christ Church Partnership

The secondary sector can really consolidate on the benefits of residential learning, especially in the transition phase, as we know that there has been huge expansion of residential experiences in the primary phase. However is opportunity being taken up? Could our secondary schools be doing more to develop this further?

The Education Endowment Foundation (EEF)[20] in its research project into the effectiveness of outdoor adventure learning claims:

Overall, studies of adventure learning interventions consistently show positive benefits on academic learning, and wider outcomes such as self-confidence. On average, pupils who participate in adventure learning interventions appear to make approximately three months additional progress over the course of a year. The evidence suggests that the impact is greater for longer courses (more than a week), and those in a 'wilderness' setting, though other types of intervention still show some positive impacts

In May 2014, the EEF produced an evaluation of a writing project[21] into how a memorable experience can enhance the writing ability of primary aged pupils. The programme increased pupils' progress by an extra nine months of schooling on average by giving pupils in their final year of primary school a memorable experience and then offering them a structured approach to writing about it. Food for thought?

Further evidence of how a school uses its programme of visits to support literacy skills is demonstrated by[22]:

Numerous trips beyond school inspire pupils to write about their anticipation of what they will see and do and their actual experiences beyond their local environment. This was seen first hand when Year 5 pupils were writing about and sharing their thoughts on what they might experience during their imminent residential trip to Eskdale.

Ofsted inspection of Barrow Island Community Primary School

This is compelling evidence to support the case for schools to develop adventurous outdoor learning programmes and to use these as part of their overall curriculum provision. If adventure based experiences create real opportunities for real learning, the challenge lies in getting message out to encourage and enable wider participation.

Ultimately, perhaps the best endorsements come from the children and young people themselves:

> *"... when we went caving I had the greatest time of my life (even more than when I went to Disneyland) ..."*
>
> Yr6 pupil - Oxfordshire Outdoors

Establishing continuity so that adventure based learning is firmly embedded into the life of the school is a challenge worth taking up, assuming the concept of a 'well rounded' education is what we are seeking?

All too often it's down to individual teachers and/or Heads to make this happen. Consistency across the board remains an aspiration, but through encouraging development of well constructed programmes, can we make it an expectation?

Perhaps it is worth going back to the group at the top of the cliff, how will their experiences be built on and developed as they move through secondary phase?

Making the case – beyond school

If we never took a risk our children would not learn to walk, climb stairs, ride a bicycle or swim; businesses would not develop innovative new products, move into new markets and create wealth for all; scientists would not experiment and discover; we would not have great art, literature, music and architecture.

Sir Digby Jones[23]

The value and benefits of adventure based learning can have a significant impact on life beyond school and this section will explore how.

The Confederation of British Industry (CBI) report First Steps: A New Approach for our Schools[24] states that 78% of employers look at attributes before anything else. The report identified these as:

The characteristics, values and habits that last a lifetime are:

The system should encourage young people to be	This means helping to instil the following attributes
Determined	Grit; resilience; tenacity Self-control Curiosity
Optimistic	Enthusiasm and zest Gratitude Confidence and ambition
Emotionally intelligent	Humility Respect and good manners Sensitivity to global concerns

The CBI has for some time claimed that a significant number of young people are not 'work ready' and that for employers:

55% say school leavers lack the right work experience and key attributes that set them up for success, including self-management (54%); problem solving (41%); and attitude to work (35%) – stressing the need for school reform to produce people who are rounded and grounded, as well as stretched academically.

If the assumption is that character is something that should be developed at school level, which now seems to be the case. It will be interesting to see if the CBI and Govt can match their respective criteria and deliver some joined up thinking. Certainly, the inclusion of adventure based learning will help meet this need for both.

Taking the employability theme further the Duke of Edinburgh's Award (DofE), in its report Under Pressure[25] identified *the transition from education to employment is difficult enough but with this added pressure, young people need to feel supported beyond their formal education to help prepare them for that first step onto the career ladder.*

It also states that for its participants (young people), *the vast majority feel under pressure to prove that they will be an 'all-rounder' in the workplace and that 83% of DofE participants think it will help them get a job* with the volunteering section being the key in helping participants prepare for the working world.

The value of volunteering is an important part of the National Citizen Service (NCS)[26] strategy, a 3 phase programme for 16/17 year olds involving a residential week undertaking adventurous activity; a planning stage designing a community project and then delivering the community project. The 2013 NCS evaluation report[27] states:

NCS improved participants' short term and long term educational and career aspirations, as well as the level of control that participants felt they had over their future success. It also increased participants' confidence in practical life skills, willingness to try new things, resilience when things go wrong, and a sense of wellbeing...

From a parental and a teacher perspective its value is endorsed as:

Most parents also thought that NCS impacted positively on their son's or daughter's life skills and aspirations. In addition, teachers felt NCS gave participants a greater sense of independence.

The Princes Trust[28] Team Programme, focussing on supporting 13 to 30 years old who are unemployed and those struggling at school and at risk of exclusion, is another example of where a residential experience is used to support the participants. Again the emphasis here is on character development through participation.

Through building their confidence and motivation, Team members are encouraged to think about their futures; this includes preparing a post-programme development plan. During the 12 weeks they:

- *Spend a week away at a residential activity centre*
- *Undertake a project based in their local community*
- *Complete a work placement*
- *Participate in a team challenge, involving caring for others*
- *Stage a team presentation, during which they recount their experiences*

In 2012 The National Trust published Natural Childhood[29], the author, Stephen Moss comments:

> *The good news is that almost everyone – parents, grandparents, teachers, health professionals, conservationists, social commentators and politicians from all across the political spectrum – agree that something needs to be done to reverse the trend towards housebound kids.*

More recently the National Trust has launched a campaign entitled 50 things to do before you're 11¾ [30] in which it encourages children to *show nature you care by getting outside and involved. Fly a kite or explore a cave, we've a list of 50 things to do with your family this summer that are sure to make nature happy.*

Another new initiative gathering momentum is the Project Wild Thing [31] launched through a film :

> *And Project Wild Thing is much more than a film, this is a growing movement of organisations and individuals who care deeply about the need for nature connected, free-range, roaming and outdoor playing kids in the 21st century.*

This is a very different approach, but equally challenging, to ensure children 'engage with the natural world'.

The Royal Society for the Protection of Birds (RSPB) launched its Get Outdoors [32] campaign, linking with Essex University to produce a method for measuring children's connection to nature:

> *For the first time, this research - reported in Connecting with Nature - reveals how connected to nature children are across the UK. The national results show that currently only 21 per cent of 8–12 year olds have a connection to nature level that we consider a realistic and achievable target for all children.*

The University of Derby Young Adventurers Award [33] seeks to discover an inspiring individual or group of young people whose passion for adventure deserves recognition.

The Council for Learning Outside the Classroom has its own awards [34], searching for outstanding contributions to outdoor learning.

The point here is that there are a growing number of external opportunities available to schools to supplement their own provision and to gain further recognition. Perhaps what is not always so clear is how to find and access them.

Making the case – the financial picture

In its Reconomics: The Economic Impact of Outdoor Recreation[35] the Sport and Recreation Alliance brings together existing information, research and evidence relating to the impact of outdoor recreation and provides a compelling case to politicians of the true value of outdoor recreation:

Outdoor recreation:

- *Is the UK's favourite pastime: three in four adults in England regularly get active outdoors.*

- *Drives the visitor economy: people spending their day enjoying outdoor recreation spent £21 billion in 2012/13 - and when you factor in overnight visits this comes to £27 billion.*

- *Creates jobs and skills: walking tourism alone supports up to 245,500 full-time equivalent jobs.*

- *Promotes a healthy nation: outdoor recreation can make a significant contribution to tackling the £10 billion cost of physical inactivity.*

So, if the educational value is not compelling enough for politicians (at both national and local levels) then perhaps the above figures will influence thinking, particularly if the connections are made through the health agenda.

Interestingly Wales has designated 2016 as a year of adventure ...

Making the case – health and welfare agenda

The contribution of adventure based activity to the health and well-being agenda should not be underestimated.

In March 2014 Public Health England launched an open consultation in support of the Government Moving More, Living More: Olympic and Paralympic Games legacy[36]. The National Physical Activity Framework, published in late 2014, with a focus on the health, social and economic costs of:

More than 4 in 10 people do not do enough physical activity to achieve good health. This is not just a personal issue, as it has significant negative impacts on the life of the individual and their communities.

The New Economics Foundation (NEF)[37] estimates the cost of a single space at a Young Offender Institution costs about £100,000 per year. Clearly, a proactive approach and preventative strategies will create significant savings if appropriately applied over a longer term.

The Prince's Trust[38] does exactly that. It supports 13 to 30 years old who are unemployed and those struggling at school and at risk of exclusion, focusing on marginalised and disengaged young people who face a range of issues and barriers in their lives. It uses the positive benefits of outdoor learning to support those who find themselves in this position.

A recent report by UK Active[39] paints a pretty grim picture of current fitness levels of young people. It calls on Government to address directly the issues of health and inactivity by creating opportunities in and beyond school. The identifiable costs of not doing anything are there to be seen, what is required is evidence of actions that are proactively seeking to reverse this.

Comparing and measuring the negative impact of doing nothing and engendering potentially anti-social behaviour patterns to the positive impact of a more self-confident, resilient young person is important. The former leads to expensive interventions, the latter to potential prosperity.

Having been involved in schemes where participants have 'turned a corner', the impact is clear to see. Instead of the criminal justice system read employment.

Making the case – further opportunities for schools

The changing face of education opens up opportunities for schools to explore different ways of developing and initiating adventurous outdoor learning programmes.

One example is the development of Adventure Learning Schools Charity[40], formed in 2009 by Professor David Hopkins, a former Chief Adviser on School Standards to the Secretary of State. Their approach is to:

> *provide a rich learning culture in which students not only meet and surpass high academic standards (especially in Literacy and Numeracy), but through the emphasis on adventure, increase their competence as learners, develop their personality and create increasingly effective learning environments for themselves as they move towards becoming citizens of our global world.*

> *Learning through adventure has a proven track record in developing just those personal qualities – independence, problem solving ability, discipline, team working and confidence – which are in demand in the modern workplace and underpin successful social development.*

There are currently three networks of Adventure Learning Schools in

The North West of England, Cornwall and Argyll and Bute. Schools in these networks meet to share best practice and benefit from regional workshops. It will certainly be interesting to see how they develop.

The advent of 'through' schools, catering for 3 – 18 yr olds offers a golden opportunity for school to develop their own longitudinal and progressive programmes. Similarly, working within partnerships offers up similar opportunities. As an example, how many secondary schools visit their feeder primaries whilst they are on a Yr6 residential? Could this be an opportunity to assist with the transition process? What would a 3-18 outdoor learning programme look like if primary and secondary linked together? More importantly, what would be the impact for students; teachers; schools; parents; communities?

King Alfred's Academy, Oxfordshire, recently appointed an Outdoor Learning Tutor to provide enhanced curriculum opportunities and support to its partner schools within its Multi Academy Trust. Its schools now offer a residential adventure based opportunities to pupils and students, using the Oxfordshire Outdoors centres. It is a statement of intent and recognition of the value of this type of work.

We are now seeing Oxfordshire Primary schools plan and deliver adventurous residential experiences across phases, with some across each year group.

The NCSL, in its Leadership for Embedding Outdoor Learning in the Primary Curriculum[41], sets out a further compelling case:

Opening up outdoor learning was seen to create a very positive and wholesome image for a school. All the headteachers interviewed reported the overwhelmingly positive feedback from their communities, echoing the experience of one headteacher:

'I've had a lot of visits from parents for next year who are from out of catchment because of what we do – it's becoming so much part of the school's ethos.'

Headteacher 1

So if the opportunities exist, how do schools make them happen?

Defining high quality in adventure based learning

Perhaps the fundamental issue for many teachers lies in determining what exactly is on offer. How the provider 'sells' itself requires visit leaders to understand and assess what this really means for their groups. Where the leader is able to determine high quality, it opens up the pathway for a powerful learning experience and positive relationships. However, this is not always the case and whether it is a good enough reason to say 'we have always done this/ gone there' is open to debate.

The Association of Heads of Outdoor Education Centres (AHOEC)[42] focusses on high quality delivery by recognising that every person has a different start point and will need support to enable them to progress and achieve as much as possible. Additionally centre staff will *design educational programmes that are based on the educational needs of individuals and the group as a whole.*

With around 150 centres in its membership, many of whom are accredited through the AHOEC GOLD[43] scheme, there exists a nationwide opportunity for teachers to access high quality provision.

In June 2015 the English Outdoor Council published a revision of its definitive document High Quality Outdoor Education.[44] This highlights 10 key outcomes of high quality outdoor learning and how such outcomes might be evidenced in an easily accessible manner. It is not designed as a qualitative research tool but offers support to teachers in recognising what the positive impacts on young people could look like. Using the indicators, simple 'checklists' identifying high quality outdoor learning could easily be developed by teachers and importantly by children and young people themselves.

In reality, deciding where to go and who to use is rooted in interpretations of what the experience should be about and what the perception of high quality really is. The challenge for teachers is to be more discerning, more questioning, more knowledgeable before committing to booking.

An exercise to help understand this:

The prospective visit leader, your colleague, asks for help and advice in comparing two providers to try and establish what high quality teaching and learning looks like.

Which of these are likely to meet your needs?

Provider A	Provider B
• Provides a set activity menu to choose from comprising up to 3 activities a day, all delivered on site	• Discusses your needs before devising and agreeing your programme
• Sessions are delivered by staff specifically trained for only that particular activity	• Most activities are off site, using the natural environment and real locations to provide real challenges
• The group sees a different person for each activity	• Group and individual aims are discussed and worked on as an integral part of the daily programme
• The sessions are instructor led, working to a prescribed 'script', often with a reduced opportunity for pupil involvement	• Activities are progressive, building on previous learning and successes / achievements
• The provider allocates staff to supervise the residential experience, especially the evenings, providing you with a 'safe haven' from your group	• Tutors mesh together the activity and environment, creating integrated learning experiences
• Your group will be sharing the venue with other schools, possibly of different age ranges	• Groups are fully involved in safety management, identifying and managing risk
	• Groups are fully involved in reviewing and evaluating their course
	• The provider uses the residential experience as an integral part of the course, requiring participants to have an input into the daily routines of the centre

Sources of advice: Outdoor Education Advisers Panel (OEAP)

As the prospective visit leader, how do you know if a provider is able to provide a high quality and safe experience? Not so long ago this would most likely have been achieved through a diverse range of questionnaires; however this would still not guarantee standards, since there was no consistency in validating the provider responses.

Fortunately much work has been done to develop this area and teachers can now easily access and obtain the advice required.

The overarching advice is available from the Outdoor Education Advisers Panel (OEAP)[45]:

OEAP members offer practical help, advice and support to staff taking children off site, to different environments including visits to local areas, museums, places of worship, visits abroad and adventure activities.

The recommendation is for LA's to have in place a person (who might still be an adviser) responsible for providing the advice, guidance, training and support necessary for delivering off site visit programmes. With the rapidly changing nature of school governance this position shifts, however it is the employer who will hold ultimate responsibility for providing the guidance and under Health and Safety law, that doesn't change.

The OEAP manages and delivers Educational Visit Co-ordinator and Leader training courses[46] for schools and other settings, which promote the safe delivery and monitoring of the quality and delivery of visits programmes. This training is available to all settings, irrespective of governance.

Critically to provide the necessary support and advice for teachers and to underpin the EVC training, the OEAP has produced National Guidance[47], a web based resource designed to balance the benefits and risks associated with the planning and delivery of visit programmes.

The National Guidance has been adopted by over two thirds of English Local Authorities plus all those in Wales. In addition it is endorsed by a wide range of professional organisations, including most teacher associations and the Guidance is 'in line with advice from the Health and Safety Executive'[48]. It is expected that the latest DfE advice (due Aug 2015) on managing visits will signpost to this Guidance.

This Guidance provides teachers with many of the answers to the questions raised around safety management of visits and it should be used in conjunction with existing school policies for visits.

OEAP, through its Outdoor Learning Cards[49] and Environmental Learning Cards, offers an easy pathway for teachers to start delivering basic experiences in their school and local environments. They are a great resource and for a growing number of schools, the starting point for their adventure learning programmes.

Sources of advice: validation and safety

> "We simply cannot afford to exclude outdoor play and learning from our children's education"
>
> Judith Hackitt, Health and Safety Executive Chair,
> Outdoor play - let our children take a risk[50]

Such a simple statement, so why does Health and Safety attract such negativity? Perhaps it's something to do with interpretation?

Unfortunately the current safety agenda is at best for teachers confusing, frequently leading to misunderstanding and doubt.

Tom Mullarkey, CEO ROSPA, stated in their publication: Planning and Leading Visits and Adventurous Activities[51] that *adventurous and challenging school visits and other opportunities for learning outside the classroom are vital to develop confidence and risk judgement among young people and to structure a society that is not excessively risk averse. Uncertainty is inherent in adventure, bringing the possibility of adverse outcome but a young person's development should not be stifled by the need to consider the worst consequence of risk, without estimating its likelihood and balancing this against the possible benefits. The concept of 'risk/benefit assessment' should be our guiding light.*

ROSPA hosts the LASER Alliance[52] (Learning about safety through experiencing risk) referred to earlier in the IHPE report, *focussing on practical, interactive scenarios teach children aged 9-11 and beyond how to deal with hazards in a fun and exciting way.* This can and does include adventure learning programmes.

So, if HSE and ROSPA are saying this teachers certainly do not need to get too hung up on the Health and Safety argument. What teachers need is clear and definitive advice, as in National Guidance.

A recent Guardian[53] roundtable discussion reported *in a recent roundtable on learning outside the classroom, health and safety regulation was barely mentioned as a barrier to outdoor learning.*

Taking this as a positive move, this section will focus on what teachers need to be looking for when considering external providers.

Visit Leaders need to understand that the external validation of providers is essential to guarantee that what the provider offers is accurate. It is also important to know the different validations that currently exist, as these will provide you with the information required at the planning stage.

There are different levels of validation and only one that is statutory.

The Adventure Activities Licensing Authority (AALA)[54] was established in April 1996 following the Lyme Regis tragedy. The Adventure Activities Licensing Service (AALS)[55] came into existence on 1 April 2007 and is presently operated by TQS Ltd, a not-for-profit company under contract to the Adventure Activities Licensing Authority (AALA).

A summary of its remit:

The Activity Centres (Young Persons' Safety) Act 1995 and the Adventure Activities Licensing Regulations 2004 make it a legal requirement for providers of certain adventure activities for young people to undergo an inspection of their safety management systems and hold a licence.

Licensing only applies to those who offer activities to young people under the age of 18 years and who operate in a commercial manner.

Generally, licensing only applies to these activities when they are done in remote or isolated places. For example, climbing on natural terrain requires a licence but climbing on a purpose-built climbing wall does not.

Licences are issued when the Licensing Authority is satisfied that the provider's management of safety is satisfactory. Inspection does not include standards of accommodation or service.

This is extremely important as it means that providers of adventurous activities must be licensed if their activities fall into scope. This is a statutory requirement and enforceable in law.

More recently, there have been significant developments for the management of non-licensable activities. The Council for Learning Outside the Classroom (CLOtC)[56] has developed the LOtC Quality Badge scheme to support validation of non-statutory provision.

The LOtC Quality Badge, awarded by the Council for Learning Outside the Classroom, provides for the first time a national award combining the essential elements of provision – learning and safety – into ONE easily recognisable and trusted accreditation scheme for ALL types of learning outside the classroom provider organisation.[57]

Crucially the LOtC Badge[58] states:

- *The LOtC Quality Badge is the only nationally recognised indicator of good quality educational provision AND effective risk management.*

- *The award of the LOtC Quality Badge indicates that the provider understands schools' needs and can tailor their offer to fit in with both current curriculum requirements and any specific requirements of the school*

- *The Outdoor Education Advisers' Panel endorse the LOtC Quality Badge and the majority of Local Authority Outdoor Education Advisers have indicated that they accept the award in place of some or all of their checks. You can view which Local Authority Outdoor Education Advisers support the LOtC Quality Badge by visiting the OEAP website.*

• *The LOtC Quality Badge reduces the red tape associated with learning outside the classroom, thereby making it easier for teachers to ensure that all children will get the opportunity to have wider educational experiences.*

The CLOtC is much more than a validating body. It offers a wide menu of training, resources and ideas for teachers.

Adventuremark[59] is another non-statutory validation for activities falling outside the scope of AALS licensing. This also validates 'schemes' eg national governing bodies

Adventuremark provides for the first time a national non-statutory safety accreditation scheme for all "scheme" or individual providers of adventurous activities. Adventuremark provides huge benefits for customers, families, groups and the providers themselves.

Using accredited providers will help people to plan more effectively adventure activity experiences that meet their needs using a system of robust accreditation which benchmarks them against standards applied throughout the U.K. It will avoid the need to seek additional reassurance.

Adventuremark inspects the non-statutory safety for LOtC and dovetails with AALS.

Most National Governing Bodies also have their own quality assurance schemes, many of which are now covered as part of the Adventuremark scheme validation.

The Association of Heads of Outdoor Education Centres[60] (AHOEC) addresses safety and quality through its own GOLD[61] inspection process, the holders of which hold the LotC and Adventuremark accreditation.

It is a confusing picture and certainly one that needs to be rationalised and pulled together to make it easier to understand. Work is going on to achieve this, but it will take time.

In the meantime take the simple view. If you were a parent would you want your child to visit a centre that holds the necessary safety / quality validation(s) or one that does not? It's a simple enough question for teachers too, so why not ask it in the planning stages.

Planning your visit – some critical questions

> *"Those running school trips need to focus on the risks and the benefits to people – not the paperwork."*
>
> Health and Safety Executive

Let's look at what a high quality adventurous outdoor experience should include.

- It should meet safety criteria, as without this a misadventure is more likely the outcome. Assuming safety is met, the focus shifts to the quality of the learning experiences on offer

- Visit leaders should have a clear vision of what they want to achieve. This is fundamental in planning a high quality experience and it is the starting point in the delivery of high quality outdoor learning. Including your group in planning from the outset is essential to the process. From experience, those leaders who do this almost always enjoy outcomes that are more positive for their groups
- Establish effective partnerships between your group and the provider, but also include any schools you might be sharing accommodation with. Again experience shows that schools with shared values and expectations will have more positive outcomes

Visit Leaders should be prepared to ask some key questions during the initial discussions prior to booking. Check with other users, do they recommend your choice of provider?

The list of questions is not exhaustive, however if the answer is NO to any it should warrant further detailed investigation:

- **Safety:** does the provider have a proven safety record? Is it accredited eg AALS; LOtC; AdventureMark. If not, why are you thinking of using it? Does the provider routinely involve your group is identifying and managing safety as a part of the activity programme?
- **Ethos:** is the provider ethos compatible with your school? Does the provider understand your visit aims? Will the provider discuss your visit aims with you and design the programme content to deliver to these? Does the provider seek to establish a partnership between the staff teams?
- **Staffing:** is the provider staff team experienced; knowledgeable and competent to work with your group? Are they mostly permanent or freelance? Do they understand and contribute to the ethos of the centre? Do they understand the ethos of your school? Can they work in partnership with you?
- **Programme content:** is the content inclusive; progressive; challenging and differentiated? Does it provide for maximum involvement and participation? Does it provide an opportunity for all participants to review and reflect on their learning and to set appropriate targets? Does it meet and deliver to your

group and individual pupil needs on a daily basis? Does the programme deliver to your stated aims?

- **Equipment:** is it fit for purpose? Does the provider have sufficient range and stock to fit your group? Are there sufficient items available, so you do not have to share?
- **Premises and facilities:** do these meet the needs of your group? If it is a residential, will you be sharing with other groups? How is this organised? Are there separate sex bedrooms and facilities? Is staff accommodation located close to your group? Are there adequate security arrangements in place to prevent intruders? Does the establishment have appropriate fire arrangements? Will the centre be suitable for your group? Are you offered a proper induction into the centre?
- **Catering:** will it meet the dietary needs of your group? Which meals are provided? How are they organised? Do meals meet with current food standards requirements? Are you able to discuss menus? Will the provider discuss specific individual dietary needs with parents?
- **Transport:** is it provided as a part of the offer? Are centre vehicles roadworthy? Are drivers licensed (and competent) to drive the vehicles?
- **Insurance:** is the provider appropriately insured? Does the provider have relevant financial procedures in place to cover cancellations and other events?
- **Finance:** does the provider confirm all costs early on? Are booking terms and conditions made clear and available? Is there a clear cancellation policy?
- **Advertising:** does the provider deliver what it says it will?

Word of mouth; familiarity and repeat visits will help the leader define what the qualitative aspect should look like. It is surprising how many times these are overlooked, often with the request for 'we will do what we did last year...' Or 'I used this provider when I was at my old school ...'

Remember who the visit is for, it could be the only chance in school life to experience such a programme, so your responsibility is to make it the best it can be.

Risk Benefit Analysis

In terms of your planning, as the visit leader, you may wish to think along the lines of a risk benefit approach. This will require different thinking, but the payoff is that it helps you put together your risk management plan and when done accurately, provides you with your risk assessments – they will be written in a different way, but they are still perfectly acceptable.

This suggestion is a part of the overall planning that you will need to establish, the detail of which is found in the OEAP National Guidance.

How it works – it's a simple equation

Use these as the headings for your visit related staff meeting(s) and accurately record the outcomes. If you include your group in all stages then you will have a more complete picture and this helps gain the compliance of all involved, as well as acceptance by parents. As you go through the process the information will provide you with a risk management plan, which forms your risk assessment

Key benefits	What are the benefits of the visit? For the group; class; school; staff? Use the benefits to drive the setting of your aims – remember to include your group in this exercise
Key obstacles	What will get in the way of you achieving the benefits? Focus on the significant issues; invite contributions from all and remember to include <u>everyone</u> who is involved in the visit, this means staff and you as well. Establish a list of 'what ifs' and once you have agreed your list (you can always add to it) move to the next stage
Actions	Having determined the obstacles, now work out what you need to do to deal with them. Identify the necessary actions; what will they look like and who will deliver them. This is the critical phase, so pay attention to detail. Double check the 'what ifs' to ensure you have covered the issues. It's worth setting some scenarios to make sure you have covered everything. One I frequently use when running training courses... During the (residential) visit you have a case of suspected appendicitis in the early hours of the morning, how do you deal with it?
Assess impact	What will be the impact of the actions on the visit? How do they relate to the benefits and to the course aims? Do you need to adjust anything? Who will be involved and do they understand what the actions should look like? How do you know they do?
Evaluate and review	Evaluate the visit. Did it meet your aims? Group aims? Was it what you expected? Did anything not meet expectations? Analyse your planning – did it deliver? Do you need to follow up on anything? Record your evaluation assessment

The 10 W's for planning your visit

Who is the visit for?   **What is its purpose?**

What are the benefits?   **Where are you going?**

When are you going?   **Which staff?**

What's the cost?   **Will anyone be left behind?**

What will the impact look like?   **Would you run this again?**

Pulling it all together, making it happen

So what is holding schools back? *The Guardian*[62] roundtable discussion reported:

> *One participant, whose school does provide plenty of opportunities for learning outside the classroom, said that schools are under a great deal of pressure to teach the curriculum and meet targets: "Every time we get an opportunity to do something, we have to sit down and look at how many lessons they are going to miss, and whether the teachers can spare those youngsters."*

Maybe this goes some way towards understanding why some schools do and some schools do not offer such programmes. However, it would be a poor outcome if this type of argument was to become the norm. The challenge is to link the learning, to be clear about the benefits and how they will support all learning.

A number of common 'problems' have been cited as potential barriers to organising an adventurous residential experience. Let's look at some of these and also some possible solutions:

Barrier	Solution
Health and Safety; copious risk assessments; ligation threat etc means it's too much trouble to organise	It requires a balanced approach – use validated centres and a risk benefit approach. Discuss with your EVC and/or Outdoor Education Adviser (or equivalent). It should not be onerous or excessive, refer to OEAP National Guidance
I don't have the skills to organise this visit myself	Talk to your EVC and to the centre providing your course. A quality centre will help support you through the whole process and help you develop your expertise and experience. The first time might be daunting, but its achievable
The centre I use doesn't have appropriate accreditation eg LOtC; AdventureMark etc	Consider again why you use it. Does it offer the quality that you should be expecting for your pupils? You will need to justify this, so spend some time thinking about it
I don't like sharing with other groups; they don't have the same standards as my school...	Talk to your provider. A quality centre will look at options with you. Consider joining with a school(s) you know and trust to have similar values. Consider using smaller centres who can cater for your needs
Costs are high; I can't bring all of my class	If eligible, consider using pupil premium and/or other local funding options eg charitable donations. If not discuss options with the centre – they may have a cheaper option at a different time of year, or can structure the course differently
I can't get time out of school; staff are complaining about pupils missing lessons	Articulate the benefits more clearly; can the course directly support other subject areas? How does the visit fit into the school curriculum plan – can it take place at a different time of year? What would the benefits of increased self-confidence look like?
Parents think it's a holiday and don't understand why we are doing this	Hold a parents evening and invite the centre to deliver a presentation to help you justify the course and the benefits it holds for their children.
I'm getting old – I don't think I can do the activities	You don't have to. A quality centre will help you work round this. Consider an 'apprenticeship' scheme to enable other staff to learn what is required – and to take some of the strain from you. Be the photographer/recorder of the experience instead
We have a new head ... my residential is cancelled so we can concentrate on academic performance ...	Set out the case that a properly planned residential experience will support and enhance curriculum performance. Invite the provider to a meeting to help present the case. Increased motivation will transfer into personal learning ...
I am told I can I can run the visit only if I cover the costs of supply	Refer to OEAP National Guidance relating to the regulations around this. It is not necessary to do this for the vast majority of residential visits
I can only run the visit with the minimum number of staff only	Refer to OEAP National Guidance. There are no set ratios, think about what staffing you need to cover the needs of the individuals; the distance you are away; the nature of the accommodation; the environment you are in; the experience of your staff team. Pose a scenario eg a pupil is taken to hospital in the early hours.... who goes? Who stays to look after the group? Who informs parents?
I will be in charge, but another member of staff will recruit the group	Not recommended! As the visit leader you should be in charge of recruitment, working within your school policies to ensure full access and entitlement

Often it is easier to let the barriers stifle rather than identify the additional benefits and create. It requires commitment to challenge and break through them, however some additional tips to help you with this:

- Consider the longer term impact, both for you as the teacher and for your pupils. Developing relationships that underpin your teaching and your pupils' learning are invaluable. They see you in a different light and likewise you see them differently. How many times have you heard colleagues talk about pupils differently as a result of what they observed during a residential experience?
- Don't forget to gather the evidence, make your own case. Think about photos; videos; recorded interviews – all of which are easily produced and could be a feature for the pupils themselves to develop and deliver. Easy to link into the ICT curriculum too.
- Factor in the CPD element too, it is an invaluable source for all staff. It just needs co-ordinating, sharing and linking. An 'apprenticeship' programme for new staff means you can develop a more sustainable staffing model.
- Manage parental expectations and ensure they see the benefits first hand. A pupil presentation to parents can be incredibly powerful; similarly to next year's cohort as a recruitment exercise. Having parents on board makes it so much easier.
- Link the residential to the school ethos and curriculum and
- Make it relevant, affordable and ensure as close to full participation as you can

These shared experiences are powerful and stimulate classroom ethos and pupil development. It is no coincidence that Oxfordshire Outdoors centres have seen an increase in primary schools booking early autumn courses, so teachers can work off the results for the rest of the school year.

Leading the programme

Your role, as the leader / organiser, is pivotal. It is certainly multi skilled and you will need copious energy and stamina to deliver the myriad of jobs associated with the role.

A quick pen picture of how your group perceives your role might reveal:

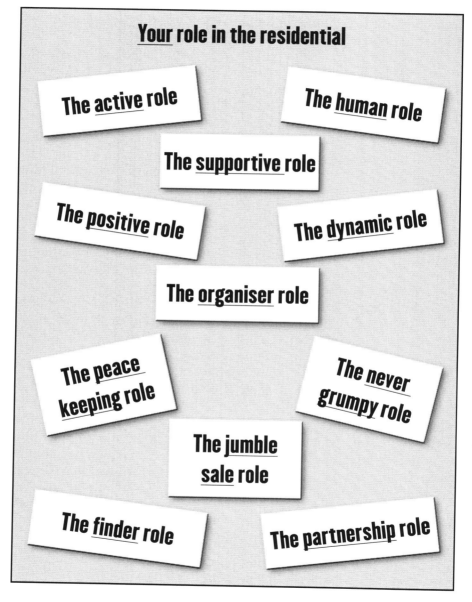

Your role in the residential

The <u>active</u> role

The <u>human</u> role

The <u>supportive</u> role

The <u>positive</u> role

The <u>dynamic</u> role

The <u>organiser</u> role

The <u>peace keeping</u> role

The <u>never grumpy</u> role

The <u>jumble sale</u> role

The <u>finder</u> role

The <u>partnership</u> role

- The active role – being out there alongside your group, supporting, cajoling, enabling
- The supportive role – helping face the challenges; knowing when and when not to intervene
- The human role – the friendly, smiling face (doesn't matter how tired you are!)
- The positive role – always, always, always
- The dynamic role – enthusiasm is your second name ...
- The organiser role – who else but you?
- The peace keeping role – who intervenes when tiredness takes over ....
- The parental role – the comforting, friendly, understanding face
- The jumble sale role – the grand master of sorting clothes; wet trainers ...
- The never grumpy role – say no more; and it's not a fixed smile, it's natural ...
- The shoe lace role – who else will tie them? Velcro is a wonderful thing ...
- The finder role – when all else fails, who finds the missing items?
- The partner role - making sure you work in partnership with the provider to maximise the learning

Is this you? Are you prepared and ready to take this on?

Author summary

It is clear that there will be no immediate, local or direct Government support for adventure based outdoor learning and the changing nature of Local Authority funding directly threatens the future of a significant number of LA funded residential Centres who specialise in this area.

If the benefits of adventure learning are to be realised then a more creative and innovative approach is required to secure provision and create the legacy for future generations.

This guide highlights where evidence exists to support adventure based residential outdoor learning programmes as powerful drivers for linking together a range of agendas including educational performance; community cohesion; health and well-being.

Can these be linked into a whole school approach to adventure learning? What might it look like for your school if you do?

Perhaps for the teacher this might be a recipe for the future, not just a wish list:

- Make the case for and establish the culture of adventure learning in your school; with staff, pupils and parents
- Develop an understanding of adventure based learning and what benefits it will bring to your school
- Articulate the benefits and link the learning strands
- Ensure that affordability and high participation become the

norm, rather than 'glossy and expensive'
- Make a residential experience an entitlement for all
- Think differently - what do you really want from your adventure learning programmes and what do your pupils really need? How can/do you make it happen?
- Work within primary / secondary partnership to develop a longitudinal offer. Why not progression from Foundation to 6th Form? Why not supported transition to the secondary phase?
- Work within your partnership structures / MAT etc to run joint courses. This can have considerable cost benefits eg coach transfer costs; maximising occupancy (an opportunity to seek incentives?)
- Invite local 'industry' representatives to see first-hand the benefits of the residential programme? Could this help your school in a different way, think sponsorship for pupil leadership?
- Celebrate your successes, in school and in your community. Don't forget the media, it makes for good reading to celebrate successful experiences, rather focus on the negative ones

It's time to join the dots and create the positive picture. Be creative, know what you want and enable those in your care to experience and enjoy real adventure. Good luck and enjoy, it's well worth the effort.

References

1. Forest School: http://www.forestschools.com/
2. National Curriculum: https://www.gov.uk/government/publications/national-curriculum-in-england-physical-education-programmes-of-study/national-curriculum-in-england-physical-education-programmes-of-study
3. Getting More People Playing Sport: https://www.gov.uk/government/policies/getting-more-people-playing-sport/supporting-pages/school-pe-and-sport-funding
4. Robin Hammerton, HMI, Ofsted http://www.slideshare.net/CLOtC/robin-hammerton-hmi
5. Ofsted Neston High Nov 2012: http://www.Ofsted.gov.uk/resources/good-practice-resource-learning-outside-classroom-neston-high-school
6. Ofsted Lavington Park: http://www.Ofsted.gov.uk/resources/good-practice-resource-improving-teaching-and-learning-using-outdoor-environment-lavington-park-fede
7. Ofsted report: The Pupil Premium: http:www.Ofsted.gov.uk/resources/pupil-premium
8. Ofsted report: The Pupil Premium an update July 2014: http://www.Ofsted.gov.uk/sites/default/files/documents/surveys-and-good-practice/t/The%20pupil%20premium%20-%20an%20update.pdf
9. Character and Resilience Manifesto: Chris Paterson, Claire Tyler and Jen Lexmond ISBN: 978-1-909274-14-3
10. Character and Resilience Manifesto: Chris Paterson, Claire Tyler and Jen Lexmond ISBN: 978-1-909274-14-3
11. DfE: https://www.gov.uk/government/news/dfe-character-awards-application-window-now-open
12. DfE: https://www.gov.uk/government/news/rugby-coaches-to-be-drafted-in-to-help-build-grit-in-pupils
13. DfE: https://www.gov.uk/government/news/rugby-coaches-to-be-drafted-in-to-help-build-grit-in-pupils
14. DEMOS: http://www.demos.co.uk/publications/character-nation
15. Institute for Health Promotion and Education: Manifesto for Safety education: http://ihpe.org.uk/2015/06/safety-education-a-manifesto/
16. National Citizen service: http://www.ncsyes.co.uk/about#
17. Outward Bound Trust: http://www.outwardboundtrust.org.uk/social-impact-report-2014.pdf
18. Paul Hamlyn Foundation, Brilliant Residentials: http://www.phf.org.uk/page.asp?id=2111
19. York Consulting: http://learningaway.org.uk/residentials/evidence/independent-evaluation-of-learning-away/

20. Education Endowment Foundation Outdoor Adventure Learning: http://educationendowmentfoundation.org.uk/toolkit/outdoor-adventure-learning/

21. Education Endowment Foundation: http://educationendowmentfoundation.org.uk/news/trial-shows-project-based-on-a-fun-day-out-boosts-writing-skills-by-nine-mo/

22. Barrow Island Community School Ofsted: http://learningaway.org.uk/news/2014/Ofsted-give-barrow-island-primary-recognition-residentials/

23. Sir Digby Jones: http://www.hti.org.uk/pdfs/pu/IssuesPaper7.pdf

24. CBI First Steps: http://www.cbi.org.uk/campaigns/education-campaign-ambition-for-all/first-steps-read-the-report-online/

25. DofE: Under Pressure – employability report: http://www.dofe.org/go/employability August 2014

26. National Citizen Service: http://www.ncsyes.co.uk/

27. Ipsos Mori – National Citizen Service Evaluation 2013 - http://www.ipsos-mori.com/DownloadPublication/1692_SRI-National-Citizen-Service-2013-evaluation-main-report-August2014.PDF

28. The Princes Trust : Team Programme - https://www.princes-trust.org.uk/about_the_trust/what_we_do/programmes/team_programme.aspx

29. National Trust Natural Childhood Stephen Moss: http://www.nationaltrust.org.uk/article-1356398566853/

30. National Trust: http://www.nationaltrust.org.uk/visit/families/50-things/

31. Project Wild Thing: http://projectwildthing.com/thewildnetwork

32. RSPB Get Outdoors: http://www.rspb.org.uk/forprofessionals/policy/education/research/connection-to-nature.aspx

33. University of Derby : http://www.derby.ac.uk/science/yaa2015/?utm_source=print&utm_medium=poster&utm_content=&utm_campaign=yaa_site&dm_i=H71,3HFPM,K07RQ9,CH5RC,1

34. CLOtC : http://www.lotc.org.uk/news-and-events/awards-for-outstanding-contribution-to-lotc/

35. SRA - Reconomics: The Economic Impact of Outdoor Recreation: http://www.sportandrecreation.org.uk/policy/research/reconomics/evidence

36. Moving More, Living More: Olympic and Paralympic Games legacy: https://www.gov.uk/government/publications/moving-more-living-more-olympic-and-paralympic-games-legacy

37. New Economics Foundation: http://www.neweconomics.org/issues/entry/criminal-justice

38. The Prince's Trust: https://www.princes-trust.org.uk/

39. UK active: http://www.ukactive.com/downloads/managed/ON02629_UK_Active_Kids_report_online_spreads_FP.PDF

40. Adventure Learning Schools: http://www.adventurelearningschools.org/

41. NCSL Research Associate Report – Leadership for embedding outdoor learning in the primary curriculum 2012: http://www.outdoor-learning.org/Portals/0/IOL%20Documents/Newsletters_Docs/leadership-for-embedding-outdoor-learning-within-the-primary-curriculum%20(3).pdf

42. AHOEC: http://ahoec.org/

43. AHOEC GOLD scheme: http://ahoec.org/about/gold-standard/

44. English Outdoor Council: http://www.englishoutdoorcouncil.org/publications

45. OEAP http://oeap.info/

46. http://oeap.info/what-we-do/oeap-training

47. http://oeapng.info/

48. http://oeapng.info/endorsements/

49. OEAP Outdoor Learning Cards: http://www.oeaptraining.info/courses/oeap/olc

50. Judith Hackitt HSE: http://www.hse.gov.uk/news/judith-risk-assessment/kidsoutdoors070612.htm

51. Tom Mullarkey ROSPA: http://www.rospa.com/schoolandcollegesafety/teachingsafely/info/school-visits-guide.pdf

52. LASER Alliance: http://www.lasersafety.org.uk/
53. Guardian newspaper article: http://www.theguardian.com/teacher-network/2012/dec/04/outdoor-learning-school-activities
54. http://www.hse.gov.uk/aala/licensing-authority.htm
55. http://www.hse.gov.uk/aala/aals.htm
56. http://www.lotc.org.uk/
57. http://www.lotc.org.uk/lotc-accreditations/lotc-quality-badge/
58. http://www.lotc.org.uk/lotc-accreditations/lotc-quality-badge/
59. http://www.adventuremark.co.uk/
60. AHOEC: http://ahoec.org
61. AHOEC GOLD: http://ahoec.org/about/gold-standard/
62. Guardian newspaper article: http://www.theguardian.com/teacher-network/2012/dec/04/outdoor-learning-school-activities

The Pupil Premium

By Marc Rowland

One of the best measures of an advanced education system is how it treats pupils who are on the margins. Great schools are a cradle for resilient, effective and confident learners regardless of their socio-economic background.

In his role as Deputy Director of the National Education Trust, Marc Rowland visited more than 100 schools across the country to discuss and review how they are using the Pupil Premium grant to improve outcomes for disadvantaged learners. This Practical Guide captures the essentials for success in narrowing the gap, and shares some examples of innovation and excellence which will be useful to other schools.

National Standards of Excellence for Headteachers

By Roy Blatchford

This Practical Guide seeks to illuminate the National Standards of Excellence for Headteachers, presenting a range of perspectives to bring the text alive for current and future school leaders and for those with the vital responsibilities of proper governance.

Part Two of the book comprises the official Standards published by the DfE, by way of handy reference. Part Three contains some short essays by school leaders.

Roy Blatchford was Deputy Chair/Chair of Drafting Group of the DfE Headteachers' Standards Review (2014). He is Director of the National Education Trust. Previously he was Her Majesty's Inspector of Schools in England, with national responsibilities for school improvement and for the inspection of outstanding schools.

The Restless School

By Roy Blatchford

What do successful schools and their leaders have in common? They are restless. There is a paradox at their core: they are very secure in their systems, values and successes, yet simultaneously seeking to change and improve. These schools look inwards to secure wise development; they look outwards to seize innovation which they can hew to their own ends and, importantly, make a difference to the children and students they serve. That is the restless school.

"In this thought-provoking book Roy Blatchford draws on 40 years of wide ranging experience within the UK and international education systems in order to capture the essence of successful schools."

Brian Lightman, Association of School and College Leaders

"Blatchford sets teachers, schools and their leaders a standard that's terrifying in prospect, yet assuredly attainable if we can just maintain our courage, commitment and determination – our professionalism, indeed, as he stresses. Inspired by this remarkable small handbook of school excellence, I don't see how we can avoid accepting and confronting the challenge. It would be rude not to!"

Bernard Trafford, Headmaster, Royal Grammar School, Newcastle

"I wish I had read The Restless School in the early days of my teaching – indeed at any stage of my teaching. In a short and pacy book I found distilled everything that matters, all expressed in a generous, open and wise way. And it puts a spring in your step."

Jonathan Smith, author of The Learning Game

Roy Blatchford is Director of the National Education Trust. Previously he was Her Majesty's Inspector of Schools in England, with national responsibilities for school improvement and for the inspection of outstanding schools.

He is the author/editor of over 150 books and is a regular contributor to the national media. Recent books include Sparkling Classrooms, The 2012 Teachers Standards and Taking Forward the Primary Curriculum.

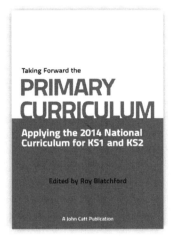

The Canterville Ghost

A Magical Musical Comedy

Peter Quilter

A SAMUEL FRENCH ACTING EDITION

SAMUEL FRENCH

FOUNDED 1830

SAMUELFRENCH-LONDON.CO.UK
SAMUELFRENCH.COM

THE CANTERVILLE GHOST

An early version was first produced by Glenn Lee on the London Fringe, January 1995. The production featured Peter Reeves as the Ghost, Josie Walker as Virginia and was directed by Steven Dexter.

The show was revised and a full-scale version was presented by Charles Stephens and Darren Ockert at the Northcott Theatre, Exeter, April 1998 and subsequently went on a national tour with the following cast:

The Ghost	Ron Moody
Mrs Umney	Nicola Sloane
Hiram Otis	Steven Wickham
Lucretia Otis	Corinna Powlesland
Virginia Otis	Sheli Andrew
Junior	Gavin Eaton
Washington	Jamie Golding
Stand-In Ghost	Paul W. Gerrard

Directed by Brian de Salvo
Designed by Will Bowen
Lighting design by Michael Odam
Illusions by Nicholas Einhorn
Sound design by Steven Hawkins
Costume design by Fizz Jones
Musical direction by James Moriarty
Musical staging by Francesca Whitburn
Orchestrations by Alan Gout

CHARACTERS

The Ghost; the dead Simon de Canterville 1525–1585
Hiram Otis; American millionaire
Lucretia Otis; Hiram's wife
Virginia Otis; their daughter, aged 16
***Junior Otis**; their son, aged 13
***Washington Otis**; Junior's twin brother, aged 13
Mrs Umney; the housekeeper of Canterville Chase
The Phantom chorus

The action takes place on a station platform and in the drawing-room, a bedroom, the ghost's chamber and main lawn of Canterville Chase, a large gothic residence in England.

Time—the present

*The roles of Junior and Washington can be made female, by altering the word "boys" to "girls" on the few occasions it comes up. The girl characters would be very tomboyish (offering a complete contrast to Virginia) so there is no reason to alter the basic characterization in any way. If female, the names of the Twins would be Brooklyn and Orlando. The lyrics on page 15 Song No. 4 Terrible Twins — **Junior**: "Will be Junior Mess" **Washington**: "Or Washington State!" should be changed to **Brooklyn**: "Will be Brooklyn the Best" **Orlando**: "And Orlando the Great!"

MUSICAL NUMBERS

ACT I

No. 1	The Tale of the Canterville Ghost	Chorus
No. 2	Welcome to England — Moving In	Twins, Virginia, Hiram
		Lucretia, Mrs Umney
No. 3	Otis Cleaning	Twins, Virginia, Hiram
No. 4	Terrible Twins	Twins
No. 5	No Ghost in History	Ghost, Chorus
No. 6	In Diff'rent Ways	Lucretia, Virginia
No. 7	An American Abroad	Hiram, Lucretia, Twins
No. 8	Lessons Must Be Learnt	Mrs Umney
No. 9	Poor Ghost	Virginia
No. 10	Poor Ghost (Reprise)	Virginia

ACT II

No. 11	The Tale of the Canterville Ghost (Reprise)	Chorus
No. 12	A Ray of Light	Ghost, Virginia
No. 13	Going Back to America	Lucretia, Twins, Hiram
No. 14	The Happy Prince	Ghost with Chorus
No. 15	Taking a Stand	Virginia, Lucretia, with Hiram and Twins
No. 16	The Spell	Mrs Umney, Chorus
No. 17	The Tale of The Canterville Ghost (Reprise)	Company

The author wishes to dedicate
the text of this musical
to the following special children

Christopher and Dougal
Sam and Jed
Ruby and Maya
Irene and Marina
Nacho, Eduardo and Mencía

*May you grow up to be happy
And live your dreams*

Also by Peter Quilter published
by Samuel French Ltd

BoyBand
Respecting Your Piers

ACT I
PRELUDE

When the CURTAIN *rises, the stage is dimly lit and full of mist*

Music

Slowly, ghoulish figures appear out of the darkness. This is the Phantom Chorus, who will make a number of appearances during the show. They are dressed in long, hooded cloaks that obscure their faces from the audience. Beneath their cloaks and hoods, each Phantom wears a wig and is made up with a ghoulish visage. They sing

No. 1 The Tale of the Canterville Ghost

Phantoms

Silence now and listen well
For a ghostly tale is due
This is the time for you
To let us cast our spell
There's the chill air of fear
And noises in the breezes
At once your warm heart freezes
At the story you shall hear.

(*Chorus*)
So, sit back, beware!
There's a spirit we can share
So let us be your host
For the tale, for the tale, for the tale
Of the Canterville Ghost!

During the following verse, each Phantom sings an individual line. As they present their line, they remove their hoods to reveal their ghostly faces and wigs

Catch your breath, if you dare
There is magic in the air
There's a whisper in the wind
And a creek upon the stair

There is shrieking in the halls
Blood is dripping down the walls
Beg for mercy from this place
Cry for freedom from the Chase.

For spells reside around here
And mystery is calling
As night is gently falling
The spectre will appear
(He will appear, he will).

(*Chorus*)
So, sit back, beware!
There's a spirit we can share
So let us be your host
For the tale, for the tale, for the tale
Of the Canterville Ghost!

There is a loud roll of thunder

With our final warning cast
From this doorway to the past
There's a ghost from whom you'll hear
In the night, he will appear.

(*Chorus*)
So, sit back, beware!
There's a spirit we can share
So let us be your host
For the tale, for the tale, for the tale, for the tale,
For the tale, for the tale, for the tale,
Of the Canterville... Of the Canterville...
— Ghost!

At the end of the number, the Phantom Chorus strikes a group pose

Black-out

The Phantom Chorus exits

SCENE 1

There is the sound of a train pulling away from a station

The Otis family — Hiram, an American millionaire; his wife, Lucretia; their twin sons, Junior and Washington, and their daughter, Virginia — enter. They are carrying a mass of luggage

The Lights come up on Canterville Station platform. A sign nearby reads "Canterville Station"

Hiram Well, kids, this is it. We're here for the whole summer!
Lucretia So, where's the housekeeper? She was supposed to be meeting us. The service here is terrible. In America, this would never happen. What's the housekeeper's name?
Hiram Umney!
Lucretia I'm sorry?
Hiram Umney. Mrs Umney.
Lucretia Really? Isn't that an awful name!?
Hiram Yes — Lucretia!
Washington I'm bored already. It's a dump. And it's freezing.
Junior It's going to rain too. Then we'll be bored *and* wet. Nice call, Pa!
Hiram I would appreciate it if you would at least give this holiday a chance. Canterville Chase is meant to be one of the finest Tudor properties in England.
Washington There isn't even a McDonald's.
Junior (*with heavy sarcasm*) Yeah — nice one, *Dad*.
Virginia I think it's going to be wonderful.
Twins You would!

Mrs Umney enters. Her housekeeping uniform is slightly Tudor in style

Lucretia Look out — something ancient is approaching.
Mrs Umney Mr Otis and family?
Hiram Yep. Are you Umney?
Mrs Umney I am Mrs Umney, the housekeeper. Welcome to the village of Canterville.
Lucretia That's a very unusual outfit you're wearing, Mrs — er — Jubbley...
Mrs Umney The uniform of the housekeeper of Canterville Chase has remained unchanged in over four hundred years.

Lucretia Really? Well, I hope you've had it cleaned! (*She laughs*) I'm
Lucretia Otis and this is my husband, Hiram.

Mrs Umney A pleasure to meet you.

Lucretia These are our two sons, Junior and Washington.

Junior Are you as old as you look?

Washington Judging by your face, you look about three hundred.

Mrs Umney Charming.

Lucretia And of course, Virginia. Named after the state where Hiram made
his first million.

Mrs Umney How delightful.

Virginia The village looks beautiful, with the fog and everything. It's kinda
strange (*to Lucretia*) I've got a feeling of *déjà vu*.

Lucretia So take a tablet! (*To Mrs Umney*) Virginia can be a little strange.
You'll get used to that. Just ignore her.

Hiram Good, well now you're here and we've all been introduced, how
about getting us out of this cold, damp weather and snuggled up in front of
a nice warm fire? Huh?

The Otis family pick up their cases. Mrs Umney stops them

Mrs Umney One moment, if you please. I must give you our traditional song
of welcome.

Junior She's gonna sing!?

Mrs Umney The custom has remained unchanged in over four hundred
years. If you please … ? (*She sings*)

No. 2 Welcome to England — Moving In

Welcome to England
To gardens, grass and trees
To fields of wheat and flowers
All blowing in the breeze
Welcome to pastures new
To manners mild and calm
Polite in tone and civilized
Welcome to your home.

It begins to rain

*The Otis family take out umbrellas, put them up and stand amidst the
downpour looking thoroughly wet and miserable*

> Welcome to England
> To blue and sunny skies
> To land of hills and valleys
> And rivers of surprise
> Welcome to customs new
> To tempers tame and cool
> Happy ways to charm your days
> Welcome to you all.

The music continues to underscore

Mrs Umney marches past. The Otis family pick up their cases and follow her off stage

There is a roll of thunder and a flash of lightning

Black-out

The Lights rise on the drawing-room of Canterville Chase

This is a typical style gothic residence in England. It consists of wood panelling and gothic arches. It has cobwebs, antique electrical lamps, a grandfather clock, a mantelpiece with various ornaments, shelves of books and an umbrella stand. There is a large portrait of the late Simon de Canterville. There is a main door and a door leading to the bedrooms. A window, US, looks out on to the main lawn. It is framed by curtains

Mrs Umney enters through the main door. The Otis family follow carrying the cases. They look around the room with awe

> I hope you will enjoy your stay
> Welcome to your home

Lucretia (*speaking*) Oh, Hiram! This house is gorgeous! It's all so —
English!
(*Singing*)   I've made up my mind
> I'm so glad to be here
> I've seen enough
> I'm happy now
> 'Cos this place is such a wow!
> I've made up my mind
> Who cares for sunshine?
> Had enough

United States
Just give me cake on china plates
You have to admit that this house here is great
So it leaves only one thing for me to demonstrate!

(*Chorus*)
We're moving in
We're now at home
We're living up, we're so refined,
It's all so old but I don't mind
We took a plane to a land in the sea
You're gonna love it, you can take it from me
Moving in, moving up, being English, being rich,
Such a thrill,
Moving in,
To Canterville.

Hiram
Lucretia
Virginia

We've made up our minds
We're so glad to be here
We've had enough
Of getting bored
Stuck in a land that's now abroad
We've made up our minds.

Twins

There's plenty to break here!

Hiram
Lucretia

Making home is now our plan.

Twins

And destroying all we can!

All

We've each got a room plus a dozen to spare —
We'll be living like kings, no worry or care!

Moving in, moving up
Being English, being rich
Taking stock, turning fate
Really rocking, going great.

Lucretia

We're moving in
We're now at home
We're living up, we're so refined,
It's all so old but I don't mind.

All (*except Lucretia*)

Moving in, moving up,
Being English, being rich
Taking stock, turning fate
Really rocking, going great.

All   We took a plane to a land in the sea
                 We're gonna love it, you can take it from me.

                 Moving in, moving up
                 Being English, being rich
                 Taking stock, turning fate
                 Really rocking, going great.

Twins   **All** (*except the Twins*)
       Moving in...   Moving in, moving up
       Such a thrill...   Being English, being rich
                                 Taking stock, turning fate
                                 Really rocking, going great

All   Such a thrill.
                 Moving in...
                 To Canterville ——

Mrs Umney   Welcome to England ——
All   —— to Canterville.

During the audience applause, a red spotlight comes up in the corner of the room creating the illusion of a bloodstain

Mrs Umney I bid you welcome to Canterville Chase.
Junior I hate the curtains.
Washington They look like someone has just thrown up all over them.
Mrs Umney They're oriental.
Hiram What's this part of the house called, Mrs Umney?
Mrs Umney The drawing-room. You may prefer to call it the sitting-room or the (*pronouncing it as "lange"*) lounge.
Hiram "Lange"?
Mrs Umney That is correct.

Hiram notices a number of ornaments on the mantelpiece

Hiram Darling, what about these ornaments?
Lucretia Oh, they're very tasteful, very refined.
Hiram I agree with you — we'll get rid of them.

The both laugh

Lucretia (*to Mrs Umney*) Are they African?

Mrs Umney French, madam.
Lucretia Yes, I thought so.
Junior (*looking at the portrait*) Who's the idiot in the picture?
Mrs Umney (*with mystery*) That's — that's ... Simon de Canterville ...
Junior Did he always dress like that or was he doing it for a bet?
Mrs Umney No, that is how he always dressed, in the mid-sixteenth century
when he was a resident of this house. And, in many ways, he still is ...

Virginia examines the stain in the corner of the room

Virginia There's a very strange mark here.
Hiram What?
Virginia Look. Here in the corner of the room. A sort of red stain.
Hiram She's right. Look! A stain! All the money I paid for this place and
I get a lumping great red stain!
Lucretia It's funny, isn't it, dear. You made your fortune from stain
removers and household cleaners, and now you've spent most of it on
renting a house that really needs them. I think it's adorable the way the
world goes round in circles.
Hiram Unbelievable!
Lucretia Why on earth haven't you cleaned it up, Mrs Bumbley?
Mrs Umney That is the Canterville stain, Mrs Otis. It has been there for many
centuries.
Lucretia Really? Well, don't you think it's time it was removed?
Mrs Umney That stain can never be cleaned, I am afraid. For it is the blood
of Lady Eleanor de Canterville. The wife of Sir Simon.
Hiram Wait a minute, wait a minute — are you telling me that I have to keep
this stain? That I have to put up with a great big pool of blood in my "lange"?
Mrs Umney If I may explain, that — is the Canterville stain. It has been a
feature of this house for very many centuries. For it is on this very spot that
Lady Eleanor drew her last breath. She was murdered by her husband, Sir
Simon de Canterville, whose portrait now looks down on his dreadful
crime. The bloodstain cannot be removed, we have tried everything.
Hiram But not — this! (*He instantly produces a bottle from his pocket and
presents it with a proud smile*) This is "Otis's Champion Stain Remover".
A fine product that will clear that stain in a matter of seconds — I should
know, I am "Otis Cleansing" — I own the company.
Mrs Umney How very American ...
Hiram Let me give you a free demonstration. (*He takes a rag from his
pocket; he sings*)

No. 3 Otis Cleansing

Otis Cleansing
For a happy ending
Otis Cleansing
We will take the strain
Stains are pending
For our bleach and no pretending
Otis Cleansing
Life will never be the same.

During the following, the Twins proceed to remove the stain with the rag and some of the ointment. The red spotlight gradually fades

There's no need to be hysterical
We have the very chemical
No spill will be resurgent
With the use of my detergent
And you'll praise the name
That cleaned the stain
That had been so offending.
Otis Cleansing,
That's my name!
(*Speaking*) Tell her, kids.

Twins ⎫ **Virginia** ⎭	Otis Cleansing For a happy ending, (ending, ending, ending) Otis Cleansing We will take the strain, (take the strain) Stains are pending For our bleach and no pretending Otis Cleansing Life will never be the same.
Twins	Otis Cleansing…
Hiram	Life is so much simpler using —
Twins	Otis Cleansing…
Hiram	Ask about our guarantee, there's —
All	Always a happy ending…
Hiram	Have a bottle as a souvenir!

On the final note, Hiram throws the stain remover to a dumbfounded Mrs Umney. The family applaud

(*Speaking*) What did I tell you!? I knew this stuff would do it.

Mrs Umney looks horrified

Virginia What's the matter, Mrs Umney? Aren't you glad the stain's gone?
Mrs Umney Indeed I am not. I fear we may all have cause to regret this act of desecration.

There is a rumble of thunder and a flash of lightning

Lucretia What a terrible climate you have here. I suppose England is so over-populated, you don't have enough decent weather to go round.

There is more thunder and lightning. The flash on this occasion lights the face of Sir Simon in the portrait. A loud evil cackle is heard. Mrs Umney screams and faints on to the floor. Hiram is shocked

Hiram Oh no! Quickly someone, help!

Junior rushes over to Mrs Umney and takes the bottle from her hand and brings it to Hiram

   Is it OK? She nearly broke the unique adjustable lid. You can't get these replaced over here.
Lucretia What did she go and do that for?
Virginia (*going over to help*) I think she fainted.
Hiram What do we do?
Lucretia Deduct it from her wages — then she won't do it again.

There is more thunder and lightning, this time very loud and bright

The room goes into a sudden Black-out

   Now what!?
Junior It's OK — I got a flashlight. (*He gets a torch from one of his bags*)
Lucretia Well, hurry up with it, I can't see a thing. Give it to me.

Lucretia switches on the torch and moves around the room with it. She moves towards Mrs Umney

   Now, where is the light switch?

She suddenly lights the face of Mrs Umney, standing directly in front of her, and lets out a scream

Mrs Umney It's only me, Mrs Otis. So sorry to have frightened you.
Lucretia What the heck is going on here, Mrs Bubbley?

Mrs Umney He's up to his tricks again. I should be used to it by now, I know, but he still manages to frighten me — even after all these years.
Lucretia Who?
Mrs Umney The Ghost, madam.
Lucretia Ghost! What Ghost?
Mrs Umney Sir Simon de Canterville.
Lucretia The guy that murdered his wife?
Mrs Umney Yes. Or as he is better known in these parts — The Canterville Ghost.
Lucretia Are you drunk?
Mrs Umney No, madam. I am quite sober and quite serious.

There is thunder and lightning. During the flashes, Lucretia's night case mysteriously works its way across and off the stage. It is pulled by a very thin piece of wire, unseen by the audience

The Lights suddenly come back on again and the stain has re-appeared

Virginia (*noticing the stain*) Well, that's strange.
Washington The stain! Look!
Junior The blood! It's come back!
Twins (*with glee*) Oh, gross!
Hiram Maniac ghosts! Recurring stains! What is all this? — I don't think you're giving us the whole picture!
Mrs Umney Perhaps it is best that I fully explain. Canterville Chase has for very many centuries been haunted by a most terrifying ghost. That of the extremely dead Sir Simon de Canterville. After murdering his wife, he disappeared in very mysterious circumstances. His body has never been discovered, but his guilty spirit still haunts the Chase. I have seen things with my own eyes that would make any Christian's hair stand on end, and many a night have not closed my eyes in sleep for the awful things that are done here. This is why we have had such difficulty in finding occupants. I believe the agents only turned to advertising in America out of desperation.
Lucretia So the place really is haunted?
Mrs Umney Oh, yes, madam.
Lucretia (*suddenly elated*) How cute! Our own little English ghost! How adorable! I must write to Agnes in Baltimore, she's already sick with jealousy, this should make her completely keel over!
Virginia So is that why you work here all on your own?
Mrs Umney Yes. Other staff tend not to stay for very long — upset by the mysterious noises and strange apparitions — but the Umneys have a long tradition in this house, going back many proud generations. So — I always put on a brave face myself.

Hiram I wondered what that expression was … Listen, Umney, we don't tend to have ghosts in the States, and even if we did, we wouldn't be afraid of them; we'd just put them into a zoo or a Broadway show.

Lucretia Or wait for them to run for governor.

Hiram So, don't you worry. Nothing yet has ever managed to frighten the Otis family! OK?

Mrs Umney Very well. I did feel it was my duty to warn you — but if you're quite sure …?

Virginia Do you think the Ghost will appear at some point?

Washington Of course he will, Virginia — what's the point of being a ghost and *not* appearing?

Junior Yeah — and when he does, Sis, we'll teach him a thing or two.

Virginia What do you mean?

Washington He needs to be shown who's in charge.

Junior Yeah — he'll be under our control. Right, Pa?

Hiram Whatever — you guys just enjoy yourselves.

Hiram begins to scrub away at the stain again, and the red spotlight gradually fades as he cleans

Mrs Umney Excuse me, but I warn you that the Canterville Ghost will not take at all kindly to any adverse action on your part. You would be mistaken to put him to the test.

Junior We're not frightened of some dusty old corpse.

Washington Yeah — you have no idea.

Junior We're your worst nightmare.

Lucretia Well, folks, I'm going to bed. All this excitement is tiring me out. Hiram? Are you coming?

Hiram (*having removed the stain*) Sure, honey.

Lucretia (*looking around*) Where's my night case? It's disappeared.

Mrs Umney I expect, madam, that the Canterville Ghost has taken it.

Lucretia The Ghost has taken my night case? Why? Is he planning to stalk the corridors wearing my nightie and a face-pack?

Mrs Umney The spirits are very mysterious, madam.

Lucretia Then I suggest you stop drinking them! Where's our bedroom?

Mrs Umney Second door on the left.

Hiram and Lucretia exit to the bedroom with a couple of cases

Miss Virginia, you might like to take the last room on the right — it's very comfortable.

Virginia Thanks.

Virginia exits, taking a case with her and pausing to stare at the portrait of Simon de Canterville as she goes

Mrs Umney The twin room is first on the right.
Junior We're not tired yet.
Mrs Umney Then I shall see you at breakfast.

Mrs Umney turns to go. The twins pull out water pistols and aim them at her back. She turns in time to catch them, grabbing an umbrella and pointing it threateningly. They back down

Mrs Umney exits, blowing the end of the umbrella like a fired pistol

Junior Get ya next time.
Washington Yeah.
Junior This is gonna be great. A real live ghost to battle.
Washington You mean — a real dead ghost!
Junior Yeah! It'll be fantastic! The question is how to do the job. Do we drench him, pelt him, hit him, trip him, dip him, or — split him!
Twins Yeah!

The Twins mime splitting the ghost in two and all his guts spilling out

Washington Hey! Why don't we do the lot?
Junior You betcha! (*Yelling*) Hey, dead guy! You're in for a real shock!
Washington You got the Otis Twins living here now!
Junior And that means ——
Twins Big — trouble! (*They sing*)

* *Please see character note on page iv*

No. 4 Terrible Twins

We'll show you
You will know
We're the best
We're the Twins
You will go
All pale and thin
Beating your chest
Shaking your head
So distressed.

Get real 'cos
You'll be scared
Off you'll fly
Through the door
You won't dare
To get us back

And it's true
You won't believe the things we'll do...

(*Chorus*)
You've never seen anything
Had a look at anything
Quite so fright'ning as the Terrible Twins!
You'll plainly be paralysed
Damaged and electrified
You will be petrified
By Terrible Twins!

We'll have you
On your knees
We're the champs
We're the Twins
You will freeze
Right on the spot
Having no chance
Blocking your ears
And wetting your pants.

Get real 'cos
You'll be fried
Off you'll run
Down the hall
You'll have died
A hundred times
When we're through
You won't believe what lives with you ...

(*Chorus*)
You've never seen anything
Had a look at anything
Quite so fright'ning as the Terrible Twins!
You'll plainly be paralysed
Damaged and electrified
You will be petrified
By Terrible Twins!

Let us begin to tell you
'Cos it will blow your mind
The things we've done all over the years
Are so desperately unkind
The Twins will be known for their rage and hate

And the damage we cause will be terribly great
The name they will give to the hell we create

Junior   *Will be Junior Mess [Will be Brooklyn the Best]
Washington   *Or Washington State![And Orlando the Great]
Twins   So pay close attention to our little song
                    We'll never get to heaven 'cos we've always gone wrong.

The music continues — "dance break". During this, Junior and Washington proceed to smash a number of ornaments and to inflict other damage on the drawing-room. Alternatively, they can do a dance routine

(*Chorus*)
You've never seen anything
Had a look at anything
Quite so fright'ning as the Terrible Twins!
You'll plainly be paralysed
Damaged and electrified
You will be petrified
Shocked and pulverized
By Terrible…Terrible…
Terrible…Terrible…
Twins… Twins.

Now that you've heard about our terrible sins
You will quake in your boots at the Terrible Twins!

Black-out

SCENE 2

Hiram's and Lucretia's bedroom

There is a door, L. There is a four-poster bed, C, and a bedside table with a small bottle on it. There is a light cord or switch above the bed

The Lights come up on Lucretia as she sits up in their four-poster bed. She holds an American magazine that obscures her face. Her face is heavily caked in the luminous green gunge that is her face pack

Hiram enters from the bathroom, wearing a vulgar pair of pyjamas

Hiram (*looking at Lucretia*) I see you found your night case, then.
Lucretia It was in the bathroom all the time — how did you know? (*She lays down the magazine, revealing her face pack*)
Hiram Just a lucky guess …!
Lucretia I hope this place manages to keep the kids occupied.

Hiram Maybe they'll love it. We could end up buying the place.
Lucretia Yes. Well, I mean, while we're here we should really buy as much
of England as we can.
Hiram It'll be good for Virginia too. A change of scene. A chance to really
find herself.
Lucretia Find herself!? You'd need a road map and Indiana Jones!
Hiram Budge over. (*He gets into bed*) At last — I could sleep for a week.
Good-night, Lucretia.
Lucretia Whatever.

They switch out the lights and settle down to sleep

*After a few moments, we hear a curious noise coming from outside the door.
It is the clank of metal and rattling chains accompanied by long, low moans
and stomach-churning elongated burps — getting gradually nearer*

Hiram? Hiram!

Hiram wakes and puts the light on

What's that noise?
Hiram I don't know, it —it sounds like it might be the "Ghost".
Lucretia (*sitting bolt upright*) The Ghost? Coming here? Into our bedroom?
For heck's sake, turn the light out — I haven't even done my hair!

*Hiram turns the lights out. There are more chain-rattling and moaning
noises*

*A ghoulish green light pierces through the frame of the bedroom door.
Slowly, the door creaks open. Swirling mist begins to fill the room. There are
eerie music and rolls of thunder and distant blood-curdling screams*

> *The Ghost enters into the room through the mist. He is dressed in a soiled
> antique gown and other ragged garments, covered with cobwebs and
> skeletons. From his wrists and ankles hang heavy manacles and rusty
> chains*

An eerie light fills the room

Lucretia buries herself behind Hiram, so the Ghost cannot see her face

*The Ghost lets out a final long moan, rolls his eyes and gnashes his teeth. He
then throws open his gown and a pile of mock human guts spring out and hang
down to the floor*

A pause

Suddenly, Hiram's face lights up and he bursts into applause

Hiram (*laughing hysterically*) Bravo! Bravo! So, you're the dead guy, right? Well, you sure got some guts!

Hiram and Lucretia laugh joyously at this comment. The Ghost is completely stunned by this reaction

Nice to meet you at last.

Ghost (*in absolute shock*) Thou darest to laugh at *me*! (*Refusing to accept that they are not completely terrified of him, he launches into a second wave of revolting ghoulishness, waving his guts at them, throwing about wild hand gestures and emitting every revolting noise in the book*)

There is no reaction from Hiram apart from a wide grin

A moment's pause

The somewhat deflated Ghost makes a final weak attempt

Boogie, boogie, boogie.

Hiram I'm sorry, I don't speak French. Anyway, I'm Hiram Otis, the new tenant of Canterville Chase. And this is my wife, Lucretia.

Seizing on a second chance, the Ghost lurches round to the other side of the bed with a loud cackle. As he is about to give Lucretia his worst, she turns sharply to look at him, revealing her green face in all its glory. The Ghost reels backwards in absolute horror

Lucretia Hi, there!

Hiram switches on the bedroom lights

Hiram That was just great. Hey, what an entrance!
Lucretia Oh!
Hiram You just kill me!
Lucretia You!
Hiram But listen, I know it's the first time we met and all, but I really need to talk to you about doing this kind of thing once we've gone to bed. I mean, we're on holiday here, right? We need to sleep and relax, right? So I've gotta insist you do something about those rattling chains.
Ghost My what?
Hiram The chains. Too loud.

Lucretia They're very rusty.
Hiram It's OK, though, we can sort this out in no time. With — this! (*He grabs a small bottle from the bedside table*) This is "Otis's Rising Sun Lubricator". Just a few squirts on that rusty old metal of yours and those chains will move around smoothly and silently. So, there you go. (*He gives the bottle to the Ghost*) Five dollars a bottle.
Ghost (*bemused*) I don't have dollars. I've got groats.
Hiram Are they painful? Anyway, look — we'll sort it out some other time. So, no more rattling chains, huh? And everybody's happy!

Lucretia smiles at the Ghost, who grimaces back

Lucretia OK? Well, Mr — Mr Corpse, we're going back to sleep now. Maybe next time we'll bring you some medication for your — for your groats. Nightie-night.
Hiram Nightie-night.

They settle back into the bed and go to sleep. The Ghost stands there, with bottle of lubricant, in total dismay. Finally, he becomes furious

Ghost I am the Canterville Ghost! I have no need of lubricant! (*He tosses the bottle to the floor and re-musters his strength, letting out an almighty moan*)

There is thunder and lightning, causing the lights in the room to flicker

The Ghost reaches his peak

Junior and Washington burst through the door wearing pyjamas designed with convict motifs and carrying pillows. They batter the Ghost violently with the pillows

The Ghost flees from the bedroom in a panic

The Twins, victorious, jump about with sheer joy. Hiram and Lucretia sit up in bed and applaud, laughing hysterically

The Lights fade to Black-out

The sound of the family's laughter echoes loudly and continually through the scene change

SCENE 3

The Ghost's chamber

It is like an old actor-manager's dressing-room, filled with costumes, props and chests. There is battered sixteenth-century throne. All are covered with thick dust and cobwebs. There are several busts and skulls. There is a stained-glass window in the centre of the back wall, which has ancient writing upon it. There is a mirror

The Lights come up

No. 5 No Ghost in History

The Ghost enters furiously. He stumbles into the room and tears off the layers of his costume, throwing them angrily aside. He catches his face in the mirror and suddenly drops from fury to dejection. He slumps into the throne

Ghost (*singing*)   No ghost in history has ever been so insulted!
No ghost in history has ever been so assaulted!
No ghost has ever been offered lubricant before!
And been attacked by little brats
With vicious acts of war
I have never known such feelings of dejection
To stand there and be battered
Leads a ghost to introspection
In my brilliant career
And my four hundredth year
I've never failed to rule
As Britain's greatest stately ghoul...

No ghost in history
Has ever been as fine as me
Cower at the things I do
Speak only when you're spooken to!
No ghost in history
Has ever been as fine as me
Frightening my many guests
And causing tremors in their chests.

I was the one who made the butler faint
As I split apart my stomach with inordinate restraint
And drove four housemaids to hysteric screams
When appearing garrotted as they dusted beams.

I was the one who on Christmas Eves
Flew across the lawn to perform "Greensleeves"
Using my bones as a xylophone
And a gangrened leg as a slide trombone.

No ghost in history
Has ever been as fine as me
Cower at the things I do
Speak only when you're spooken to!
No ghost in history
Has ever been as fine as me
Blasting all the world with fear
And then I simply disappear.

But though my actions have raised violent storms and
        thunder
And put folk in fear of what lies six foot under
All the world means nothing
If I find myself to be
No longer driving fear and dread
Into those who witness me
When a ghoul can't rule
From his tomb with a view
It's a truly grave situation
What's a ghost to do?

(*Speaking with renewed defiance*) Do? — I'll tell you what I'll do! Ha!
Unfearing Americans! I'll show them! I'll have them gibbering
uncontrollably before the week is out! For am I not Sir Simon de
Canterville — the finest spook that ever — died! My hauntings are
triumphant! All my personas, my characters, the very stuff of graveyard
legend!

*During the following, as he mentions each of his famous personas, a
member of the Phantom Chorus appears in the character's guise mentioned. Each appearance is surprising, they emerge from trunks, door-
ways, through portraits, from beneath flooring, from behind curtains*

Music continues to underscore

(*Speaking*)   There was Dreadful Desmond, the Deadly Dancer;
                    Ghastly Gareth, the Garrotted Gallivant;
                    Calamity Carol, the Cannibalistic Cook;

        Malicious Martin, the Murdered Musician;
        Petrifying Peter, the Pulverizing Peasant;
        Beelzebub Brenda, the Bludgeoning Barmaid;
        Firesome Freddie, the Fearsome Fop;
        Hatchet Harriet, the Horrifying Harlot;
        Tortured Titania, the Terrifying Tart
        And of course —
        Wretched Robert, the Revenging Rector!

All of the Phantoms are now on stage, dressed as each of Sir Simon's past triumphs. They join in the rest of the song with the Ghost; singing

All   No ghost in history
        Has ever been as fine as me
        Cower at the things I do
        Speak only when you're spoken to!
        No ghost in history
        Has ever been as fine as me
        Gnashing teeth and dagger claws
        And then I pause for my applause

In the verses that follow, lines are divided amongst characters within the Phantom Chorus

Wretched Robert   I was the one who made the rector holler
        When grinning at his face in a clerical collar

Calamity Carol   And caused a duchess to spill her tea
        And then fall into her porridge at the sight of me

Dreadful Desmond I am the one who at every chance
        Has led each guest through a merry dance

Beelzebub Brenda For a ghost who's great won't accept defeat

Ghastley Gareth   Take any chance for a fast retreat!

All   No ghost in history
        Has ever been as fine as me
        Cower at the things I do
        Speak only when you're spoken to!
        No ghost in history
        Has ever been as fine as me ——

Ghost   I'll have them fearing for their souls
                       As I employ my many roles
                       And when I've crushed those guttersnipes
                       I'll tear apart their stars and stripes!

All   I will show them
                       With all my heart
                       That no ghost in history
                       Has been...so...smart...!

They form a final triumphant pose

Thunder and lightning

Black-out

SCENE 4

The drawing-room. The next morning

The drawing-room is set for breakfast. There are a table and some chairs. There is a chair set in a corner of the room for Virginia. There is a tea-trolley with bowls, jugs of water, teacups, a tureen of porridge, a pot of tea and a milk jug

As the Lights come up, Virginia is looking around the room

Mrs Umney enters

Virginia Good-morning, Mrs Umney.
Mrs Umney Good-morning, Miss Virginia. What may I fetch you for breakfast. Toast? Or a little porridge?
Virginia I don't know... What do you suggest?
Mrs Umney I myself always have porridge. It warms you through and gets your bowels moving. Great Britain stands or falls on porridge.
Virginia Then I guess I better have that. But, I'll wait for the others.
Mrs Umney Very good. I think we might be lucky and have some sun later on.
Virginia That would be great — I'd like to do some painting.
Mrs Umney I trust you have no objection to eating in the drawing-room. The breakfast room is still gorged with blood from a haunting episode several years ago. We just don't seem to be able to scrape it all off.

Virginia You need a good scourer. Talk to Pa, he has plenty.

Lucretia enters

Mrs Umney Morning, Mrs Otis. Will you be having breakfast?
Lucretia Just coffee.
Mrs Umney I'm afraid we don't have any coffee. Could I interest you in Earl Grey?
Lucretia That depends — is he attractive? (*She laughs*)

Mrs Umney just waits for an answer

Just give me something hot in a cup with sugar in it! And a cookie!

Mrs Umney exits to fetch the biscuits

Virginia Morning, Ma.
Lucretia Hey, did you hear about last night? Boy, did those twins give the ghost a seeing to. It was a riot — your father is so proud of them. You should have been there.
Virginia I don't want to spend my holiday attacking people!
Lucretia He's not people — he's a ghost! At least Junior and Washington have found an activity for the holidays — rather than just slouching around.
Virginia I'm not going to slouch, I'm going to paint.
Lucretia Paint?!
Virginia I enjoy it.
Lucretia Then do it. What do I care?
Virginia Well, you just don't care, do you, Ma.
Lucretia Of course I do. It would just be nice if you joined in with everybody else. But that's you — always on the sidelines. Thinking rather than doing.
Virginia That's not fair.

No. 6 In Diff'rent Ways

Lucretia (*singing*) Why did you shrink when all others laughed?
You always think — I mean, that can be daft
Not a single retort
Just sensible thought
And some of the clothes you've bought!
There's a world out there
But you don't seem to grasp it
Be brave and try
Or life will pass you by.

(*Speaking*) And it passes quickly — believe me, it goes like a train sometimes.

Virginia (*singing*) I wish that you could see
                    There's some good here in me
                    I'm trying to please.
Lucretia (*speaking*) How are you trying?
Virginia (*singing*)You can hate me if you feel you should
Lucretia (*speaking*)We don't hate you, Virginia.
Virginia (*singing*)Being diff'rent isn't good.
Lucretia (*speaking*)Well, it's not very helpful.
                    (*Singing*)   Why must you walk when all others run?
                                  You never talk — I mean, that can be fun!
                                  Not a single complaint
                                  Acting like a saint
                                  You just sit there and you paint
                                  There's a world out there
                                  But you don't seem to grasp it
                                  Be brave and try
                                  Or life will pass you by.

Lucretia (*singing*)	**Virgina** (*singing*)

Why must you walk
          when all others run?
You never talk —
          I mean, that can be fun!
Not a single complaint
Acting like a saint.
You just sit there and you paint
There's a world out there
But you don't seem to grasp it
Be brave and try
Or life will pass you by
	I wish that you could see
	There's some good here in me
	I'm trying to please
	You can hate me if you feel you
	          should
	Being diff'rent isn't good.

Both   Diff'rent ways
                      Just diff'rent ways
                      Looking at life
                      In diff'rent ways.

As prior to the bridge, the next two sections are sung in counter melody at the same time, but with Lucretia and Virginia exchanging melody lines

Virginia	**Lucretia**
Why can't I do what feels right inside?	I wish that you could see
I never have sense that you've any pride	You could be just like me
What I say isn't right	By taking a stand
Should I stand up and fight	Just be passionate about some thing
If it's just for your delight?	Think of all that that could bring.
There's a world out there	
In my way I can grasp it	
I'm not strong but I	
Like life passing by.	

The music continues to underscore

Lucretia I'm just waiting for the moment that you grab life by the throat and show us you have the family spirit.

Virginia And be just like the rest of you? You think that's a good thing?

Lucretia It depends how you look at it.

(Singing)	Seeing life in diff'rent ways...
Virginia	Seeing life in diff'rent ways...
Both	Seeing life in diff'rent ways...

Hiram (*off*) Hey, are you ready for my heroes in there?

Lucretia Bring in my babies!

Hiram enters smoking an enormous cigar. The Twins, also smoking enormous cigars, and Mrs Umney carrying a plate of biscuits follow him

Hiram Here you go, guys — ready for a well deserved breakfast? What do you want?

Junior I want doughnuts — and hash browns!

Washington Waffles and pancakes!

Junior Hot dogs, burgers and a turkey leg!

Mrs Umney Porridge for breakfast, boys?

Junior What!?

Mrs Umney Porridge-oats and a little water.

The Twins mime throwing up

Twins (*mimimg*) Bleeurghgh!

Mrs Umney And let me get rid of these for you. (*She takes away the Twin's cigars and drops them into the jug of water*) We don't want to catch nasty diseases, now. (*She takes Hiram's cigar as well*) Do we, Mr Otis?

Hiram Umm — no.

Mrs Umney There. That's better. (*She places Hiram's cigar into the jug of water*) And what can I fetch the Master of the House for breakfast?

Hiram I thought *you* had already eaten!

Mrs Umney Some lovely porridge?

Hiram No, I'm not hungry. Just a drink.

Mrs Umney Tea?

Hiram I suppose so.

Mrs Umney Assam, Darjeeling, Orange Pekoe?

Hiram No, just the tea.

Junior This is unbelievable! Oats for breakfast!

Lucretia Don't complain, she came with the house.

Washington So did the woodworm.

Mrs Umney If anyone needs me —(*to the Twins*) I'll be poisoning the milk!

Mrs Umney exits with the milk jug

Junior Come on, Pa — tell us we don't have to eat this garbage.

Virginia You should try it, it's really nice.

Twins Shut up!

Virginia, upset, takes a seat in the corner of the room and reads a book

Junior We need some decent food, Pa. That old hag is trying to kill us with this stuff. And she really, really hates us.

Washington I mean it's like a joke — they don't have anything American here.

Virginia Then try something English.

Washington I don't want to! I hate the English. They're so pompous.

Junior And so poor!

No. 7 An American Abroad

Hiram (*singing*) Cultured New Yorkers
Of a quite superior class
Find the habits of the European poor
A superior pain in the ass
But we rise above society
In the only way we can
That's the Otis way
And I intend to stay
An abroad American.

An American abroad
Makes his stamp on the English soil
As we foil their plans
With our tough demands
And the titled types recoil
An American abroad
Putting up with the English drawl
There's no buckwheat cakes
And we miss big steaks
And the mighty urban sprawl
So God bless America
Where we all stand to gain
We'll amaze this place
With a stateside grace
Or we'll slowly go insane.

Lucretia
Hiram

We lost our tempers in Cairo
Our digestion in Bombay
And we never found either again
So we packed our bags and made our way

We can buy culture tomorrow
So why waste time today
With money, there's no need for class
And on history we're glad to pass.

Hiram
Lucretia
Twins

Americans abroad
Making stamps on the English soil
As we foil their plans
With our tough demands
And the titled types recoil
Americans abroad
Putting up with the English drawl.

Junior
Washington
All

There's no doughnut gems
We want M & M's
And the mighty urban sprawl
So God bless America
Where we all stand to gain
We'll amaze this place
With a stateside grace
Or we'll slowly go insane.

Hiram   When I was too young and foolish
                       Cash was all I would pursue

Twins   He thought it the important thing in life
Hiram (*speaking*) Too right!

  (*Singing*)   Now that I'm old I know it's true
  (*Speaking*)   As I have seen down in Miami
                       Pretty models can earn their fill
                       Though millionaire models are rare enough.
  (*Singing*)   Model millionaires are rarer still.

All   Americans abroad
                       Making stamps on the English soil
                       As we foil their plans
                       With our tough demands
                       And the titled types recoil (recoil)
                       Americans abroad
                       Putting up with the English drawl
Junior   They've got meadow larks
Washington   But no Disney parks
All   And no mighty urban sprawl
                       So God bless America
                       Where we all stand to gain
                       We'll amaze this place
                       With a stateside grace
                       Or we'll slowly go insane.
                       We'll slowly go … insane …

During the audience applause, the stain reappears and glows yellow

During following, Mrs Umney enters

At the end of the song, the family ends up standing in the vicinity of the Canterville stain

Hiram Has that stain come back?
Virginia Yes, it has.

Hiram examines the stain

Hiram It's kind of yellow this morning. Very strange.
Virginia Pa, could I have some money to buy some paint today? I'd like to
   do some pictures, but some of the colours are running out.
Junior Oh, please.

Washington Is she serious?

Lucretia Apparently.

Hiram We'll have to see how we do in the village. We're in the middle of the countryside here. You might only be able to buy fertilizer.

Junior (*to Washington*) Come on, let's start making plans.

Washington Right!

Lucretia Plans for what?

Junior We want to really teach the Ghost a lesson next time.

Virginia Why don't you just leave him alone? That poor old Ghost has been here all these years and now we arrive and all you wanna do is attack him. It's not right. He might have tried to scare us a bit, but we should at least make an effort to be friendly.

Washington Hallo! He's a spook, Virginia! A dead guy! What are we supposed to do? Invite him for breakfast?

Virginia I think that would be great. We've never had breakfast with a Ghost before — it might be interesting.

Junior I can't believe you're my sister!

Virginia Neither can I.

The door bursts open and there is a loud crash of thunder

The Ghost enters. He is dressed in another ghoulish disguise and brandishes a large axe

Mrs Umney and Virginia hide themselves in corners of the room, but Hiram and Lucretia just look unimpressed

The Twins rush off

Ghost Oh, I know I don't frighten you colonials — I'm just some fool of a spook! But the axe is real!

Lucretia Oh, cut it out!

Ghost I'd rather cut it off! This axe has cut off a hundred human heads and caused the Ghost of Anne Boleyn to walk the Bloody Tower! So let's have a little scream for once shall we? Come on! Just a hint of terror?

The Twins enter behind the Ghost. They are each covered in a large white sheet, and carrying a scythe. They approach the Ghost and make ghoulish noises

The Ghost turns. On sight of the apparition, he immediately screams with fright, drops his axe and runs off. Just as he exits, he trips and his departure is accompanied by a medley of tumbling thumps, crashes and screams

Hiram Well, I guess he found the stairs!

Uproarious laughter from Hiram and Lucretia. The Twins remove their disguise and jump with joy at their victory

Come on, guys, I'm gonna take you into the village for a real heroes' breakfast.

The Twins cheer

You coming, Virginia?
Virginia No, I'm not.
Hiram Suit yourself.

Hiram, Lucretia and the Twins exit

Virginia Poor ghost ...

Virginia exits, sulkily

Mrs Umney begins to clear away breakfast

After a moment, the Ghost enters behind Mrs Umney. He is not seen by her. He looks bereft and exhausted. Spotting Umney, he approaches her

Ghost (*yelling into Mrs Umney's ear*) Boo!

Mrs Umney screams with fright, dropping some of the things on the floor

Do I frighten you!?
Mrs Umney (*terrified*) Yes! Oh, yes!
Ghost Are you sure?
Mrs Umney Quite sure.
Ghost Why?
Mrs Umney You're hideous and terrible.
Ghost Thank you. So why don't I frighten these Yankee Doodles!? This is a disaster! It is all very well for you. You can continue with your duties as your mother and grandmother did before you. But I have been usurped in my efforts. I am compelled to scare all tenants from this place — such is my duty and the nature of my punishment. But am I to be continually thwarted by this abominable family of a lubricant salesman? Am I to spend the entire summer at the mercy of tourists? Having my incarnations dressed down and my stain scrubbed up? I am the Canterville Ghost! The most feared spirit in England! I have been attacked, battered and degraded, humiliated and mocked — more than any phantom could ever expect to endure.
Mrs Umney (*quaking*) It must be very disappointing for you.

Ghost Disappointing!? It's beyond belief! What possible explanation on earth can there be for this family? — Hm!?

Mrs Umney Well, they are American — the culture is very different; they have no ruins, no curiosities ...

Ghost No ruins? No curiosities? They have their navy and their president! I have utilized every ounce of my fearsome talent — and look at the result.

Mrs Umney Perhaps you should take some time off? You might — retire?

Ghost Oh a fine prospect! Spending the rest of eternity sitting in silence in a dark chamber, reminiscing about my degradation. Ageing not one day as layer upon layer of dust settles on my tear-wet cheeks and the air fills with the decay of the world and the misery of failure. I'll pass on that one, if you don't mind! Well? What have you got to say for yourself now?

Mrs Umney Nothing, nothing... I — I was just thinking, I really need to — to — clear up breakfast ...

Ghost Oh. Well, let me give you a hand.

Accompanied by a revolting sound effect, the Ghost wrenches off his hand and gives it to Mrs Umney. (The Ghost has the fake hand hidden up his sleeve. He brings it out, while pulling his real hand up into his sleeve.) Mrs Umney screams. The Ghost laughs

And there's plenty more like that up my sleeve! Aha (*He brings his real hand back*) I must say — for me, Umney, you are a real tonic.

Mrs Umney I'd rather have the gin!

Ghost Ah, Umney. Just like thy mother, and her mother before. All of them grabbing the mead and quaking with terror as part of their devoted service. There's nothing like having an Umney around when you fancy a scream or two. And so — I am once again filled with spirit! So, to business. Prepare yourselves, my transatlantic friends. (*He hunches his back and limps across the stage*) For soon I shall return with my most terrifying apparition yet — and you'll be screaming "A hearse! A hearse! My kingdom for a hearse!" The battle may have been lost, but the war is not over yet!

Thunder and lightning

The Ghost exits with a flourish

Mrs Umney clutches at her heart and leans weakly against the wall. After a moment, she pulls herself together and proceeds to clear up all the mess

Virginia enters

Virginia Was that you screaming?

Mrs Umney No, no — just clearing my throat.
Virginia I'm so sorry, Mrs Umney.
Mrs Umney About what?
Virginia My family. They've been very cruel to the ghost and I — I'm just really sorry.
Mrs Umney Don't feel sorry for the Canterville Ghost, Miss Virginia. In his own turn, he has been responsible for petrifying many people. Myself included.
Virginia But that's his job, isn't it?
Mrs Umney Well, that's one way of looking at it! Forgive me, but it is very unusual to hear someone taking the Ghost's side.
Virginia I feel sorry for him. But I'm glad he has you here.
Mrs Umney Oh, I *have* to be here! But on days like this, it is most difficult! The Ghost is bad enough, but your family — I frankly admit — are driving me to distraction! They have to discover the true values of life.
Virginia Values?
Mrs Umney Values are an Umney tradition. They have been up-held by my family for over four hundred years. (*She sings*)

No. 8 Lessons Must be Learned

For generations we have served
And so we got what we deserved
But who am I to break the chain?
I'll simply take the strain
I'll hold the secrets of this house within my heart
And do my duty, always play my part
But at times like these,
You have to admit
The strong desire
To scream and quit.

The mess here, it chills me
Their attitude just kills me
Could anybody ever praise
The way they choose to live their days?
I can't be *compos mentis*
Now, I've lost my thread —
But what I meant is ...

Lessons must be learned, my dear
We have to grow, and that is very clear
For modesty's a prize and vanity's a bore

It's such a chore when they seem deaf to your cries
They must learn to care.
A selfish life is such a strain,
Humanity goes down the drain
Respect and love are priceless gifts
That we have chance to earn
In lessons we learn.

To mend and cook and always clean,
That is the way it's always been
But how am I to tend these "yanks"
Who are so short on thanks?
I'll tame the twins within this house
Just give me time
Though having brats like these is certainly a crime.
But there's a chance to improve, a chance to repent,
And not waste time causing discontent.

Lessons must be learned, my dear,
We have to try and that is very clear
Humility is good,
But avarice is bad
It's very sad when they don't hear as they should.
They must learn to care,
Accepting people as they are
Is really fine and not bizarre
Respect and love are priceless gifts
That we have chance to earn
In lessons we learn.

A greedy life is not admired
It leaves you feeling sad and tired
Respect and love are priceless gifts
That we have chance to earn
In lessons we learn ...
Lessons we learn ...
Lessons we learn ...
(*Speaking*) I'm just showing concern.

Virginia But I still don't understand why you stay here.
Mrs Umney This was my mother's position. And her mother's before. And
so it goes on; the Umneys have been housekeepers here for centuries. It is
our heritage. Our duty. Besides which, the day may come when the
Canterville Ghost is in need of me — and I will be the only person on earth
who can help.

Virginia I don't understand.

Mrs Umney It's very complicated. But to put it simply; one day the Ghost may find the pathway to his freedom. Until that day, he is compelled to remain here, to haunt and frighten and disturb. If, by some chance, that day arrives when he may become free to leave this earth, then there are certain ceremonies that are necessary.

Virginia Ceremonies?

Mrs Umney Don't let it concern you, my dear. The point is that the knowledge of all this has been passed down from mother to daughter for hundreds of years. How could I leave? How could I betray four hundred years of dedicated housekeeping service? And four hundred years of trust?

Virginia You sound very brave to me.

Mrs Umney Not brave; stubborn.

Virginia The Ghost's apparitions are very good, aren't they?

Mrs Umney They are legendary. Most people are quite frightened out of their wits. Though you are the first Americans to stay here — and he does seem to have hit a bit of a glitch.

Virginia We sort of see things differently, I guess.

Mrs Umney Yes. The poor Ghost must be quite beside himself.

Virginia "Poor Ghost"? Do you think he's unhappy? I think he must be. He must be miserable.

Mrs Umney If he is, there's really nothing we can do about it. There, everything cleared up. I must go and start cleaning the rest of the house now.

Virginia OK.

Mrs Umney It was very nice talking to you. And don't you worry. Just enjoy the sunshine.

Mrs Umney exits, carrying most of the broken items

Virginia wanders over to the portrait and stares at the portrait of Sir Simon de Canterville. The Lights close in on Virginia and the portrait

No. 9 Poor Ghost

Virginia (*singing*) All my family seem to view
This poor ghost as a joke
And yet I can't help wondering
If he needs some help from me
I have watched the days go by
And seen this figure come to us
But I never felt afraid
Of all his haunting games

Somewhere in my heart there beats
A feeling I should go to him
And ask him if a shy young girl
Can help him change his world...

Are you lonely, poor Ghost?
Are you sad?
Where are you hiding now?
Do you need me?
Are your dreams, poor Ghost,
A wish you can't allow?
Are you weeping, poor Ghost?
Dry your eyes
And find a path from hell
Can you hear me?
Hear my voice, poor Ghost?
Break your life from this spell.

Is your soul so lost of love
That all these years have passed in hate
Is there no answer to your pain
And why you must remain.

Are you lonely, poor Ghost?
Are you sad?
Where are you hiding now?
Do you need me?
Are your dreams, poor Ghost,
A wish you can't allow?
Are you weeping, poor Ghost?
Dry your eyes
And find a path from hell
Can you hear me?
Hear my voice, poor Ghost?
Break your life from this spell.

Where is the place you sleep in?
Is it dark with all your fears tonight?
You've lost a land of sunshine
Try to find the light...

There are secrets here I know
There's some magic in the air
Dare I look to find the answers
So lost in his despair?

Are you weeping, poor Ghost?
Dry your eyes
And find a path from hell
Can you hear me?
Hear my voice, poor Ghost?
Break your life from this spell

The Lights fade to Black-out

SCENE 5

The drawing-room. The following evening

The Lights come up. The stain in the corner of the room is blue

*The Twins are in the midst of preparing a series of elaborate traps, including
a tripping rope and some buckets of water. The room begins to resemble an
army assault course. Hiram is reading a New York newspaper in the
armchair*

Lucretia enters

Lucretia I hope you two are being careful.
Junior Yes, Ma.
Lucretia Let's hope you finally get rid of him this time.
Hiram (*folding his paper*) Where's Virginia?
Lucretia Painting the trees.
Hiram What?
Lucretia Don't say a word, I don't want to hear it. She's your daughter, you
    must have filled her head with these things.
Hiram Painting trees?
Lucretia Didn't I just say I don't want to hear about it? And it gets worse
    — they're purple trees.
Hiram Well, that at least shows originality.
Lucretia Don't push it, Hiram. The girl continues to malfunction and you
    don't do a thing about it. Look at our wonderful sons, what valuable use
    they make of their time.
Washington Thanks, Ma.

There is a roll of thunder in the near distance

Junior Hear that, Washington?
Washington Yeah, he must be on his way.
Junior This is gonna be great! Everyone over forty; get the hell out of here.

Hiram Good, I can go eat.
Washington You too, Ma.
Lucretia I'm nowhere near forty.
Junior Sure, Ma.
Lucretia Besides, I want to stay and watch.
Junior It's not for grown-ups, it's too dangerous.

There are the distant sounds of ghostly moaning and chain rattling

Washington Shsh! That's him — he's coming already! Quickly, clear the
room!

Junior tries to hustle his parents from the room

Junior Go! Go! Come on, move it!

*Hiram and Lucretia are ushered out, but watch all the action peering in from
the edge of the room. The Twins get ready*

*The moans get louder. More thunder and lightning is heard. There is a flash
of green smoke*

> *The Ghost appears as though out of nowhere striking a fearful pose. He is
> dressed in a seventeenth-century costume with a ruffled neck — and no
> head! His head is tucked under his arm. (The costume is made so that the
> "shoulders" are raised above the actor's head. This is most simply done
> by the actor wearing a sort of hat that forms the shape of shoulders within
> the costume. He is therefore completely immersed in the body of the
> costume and can appear headless. The head in his arms is made of papier
> mâché or a football.) He parades about the room, moaning. His voice has
> a resounding echo*

Ghost Beware all who might chance their fighting spirit against a frightening
spirit! For this is my persona of Dreadful Damien and it comes with powers
that would chill the blood of any mortal. For Damien had his head untimely
ripped from his shoulders and no man since has stood more than a moment
in his company without crumbling to their knees in tortured agony. Doesn't
this sight fill you with horror!? Behold the thunder!

There is the sound of thunder

Behold the screams!

There are sounds of screams

Behold the mists of hell! Behold the —— !

Junior Now, Washington!

Washington karate kicks the model head, sending it flying into the air. Junior catches the head and runs about the room as though he is playing in an American football match. The head is passed continuously between the joyful Twins as the remainder of the Ghost's body staggers about the room trying to retrieve it

Ghost This is just too much! Give me back my head at once!

Washington drop kicks the head and it flies off stage through the door

   The Ghost exits in pursuit of his head

Everyone laughs and applauds wildly

Junior That was just the best!
Washington Did you see him running around? What an idiot!
Junior What did you think, Pa?
Hiram Fabulous!
Lucretia We're gonna get you both in the team next year.

   Virginia runs in

Virginia What happened? What's been going on?
Junior Attack number two; a major victory.
Virginia Why are you doing this? Leave him alone!
Washington Oh, great, Virginia's on the Ghost's side.
Lucretia What's the matter with you? Pull yourself together!
Virginia It's wrong.
Lucretia You're wrong.
Virginia Ghosts have feelings too.

The Twins burst into hysterics at this comment

Hiram (*looking off*) Hey, quiet, boys, quiet! He's coming back.
Junior Phase two!

The Twins pull the tripping rope across the floor and then crouch down holding buckets of water which they are ready to throw at the Ghost. However, the Ghost waves a white handkerchief into the room to signal surrender. He follows this with a small British flag and then an American one. The Twins put the buckets down

The Ghost enters. His real head has now emerged from the costume or he is wearing something else. He looks thoroughly dejected

Ghost I have something to say. Never, never have I felt quite so low and degraded. And never in my four hundred years have I felt so middle-aged. It is quite clear to me that England was wise to get rid of her colonies. As I take it, that you yourselves have no intention of leaving here, I myself shall take leave of you. (*Choked with sorrow*) I shall retire from my duty, revert to my chamber, and leave you in peace. And I trust you will do me the courtesy of leaving me to cry in solitude. Enjoy your victory. (*He turns to go, then turns back again*) And just for the record — I would like you to know, that many people in the past have considered me to be quite a fine Ghost. I am sorry to have let them down, and to have let myself down, quite so badly... now, please allow me the little dignity of simply *walking* down to my chamber ... I am quite out of magic today.

The Ghost limps slowly off, his head bowed, his arms hanging weakly at his sides

Virginia walks forward and stops for a moment

The Lights change and the action, apart from Virginia, freezes on stage

No. 10 Poor Ghost (Reprise)

Virginia (*singing*) Are you weeping poor ghost?
　　　　　　　Dry your eyes
　　　　　　　And find a path from hell
　　　　　　　Can you hear me?
　　　　　　　Hear my voice poor ghost?
　　　　　　　Break your life from this spell.

Virginia runs out of the room, using the same exit through which the Ghost departed a few moments earlier

The Lights fade to Black-out

The CURTAIN *falls*

ACT II
SCENE 1

The Ghost's chamber

There is a large leather-bound book behind the throne

When the CURTAIN *rises, the Lights are dim*

During the following song, the Phantom Chorus emerge slowly, from every hidden corner and crevice of the chamber, as the same characters as Act I Scene 3.

No. 11 The Tale of the Canterville Ghost (Reprise)

Phantoms
Silence now and listen well
For our tale is not yet through
There's much more time for you
To let us cast our spell
Soon the air fills with fear
And noises in the breezes
So halt your coughs and sneezes
At the story you still hear.

So, sit back, beware!
There's a spirit we can share
So let us be your host
For the tale, for the tale, for the tale
Of the Canterville Ghost.

Each sings an individual line in the two-part verse that follows

Though the Ghost had a plan
This new family never ran
There is trouble now afoot
And he's done the best he can
Is his ending drawing near?
Will he never more appear?
Is he lost in his disgrace
In the dungeon of the Chase?

But all is not resolved yet
For mystery is calling
And when all seems appalling
The magic will appear
(It will appear, it will).

So, sit back, beware!
There's a spirit we can share
So let us be your host
For the tale, for the tale, for the tale, for the tale,
For (the Canterville) the tale, for the tale, for the tale,
Of the Canterville... Of the Canterville...
— Ghost!

On the final note of the song, all the figures vanish quickly from view

The Lights change. Golden Lights come up on the stained glass window and highlight ancient writing. It reads: "When a golden girl can win, Prayer from out the lips of sin"

The Ghost enters, looking exhausted. He slumps in to his throne

Ghost Gad's blood! There must be something here, some way to lift the curse. Something I've missed, some ancient spell, lost in time. Latin incantations; *"Mirabili Dictu; "Mutatis Mutandis." "De Profundis",* *"Annus Horribilis"* — honestly! Who'd ever use a phrase like that! Oh, this damn book! And this damn prophecy! "When a golden girl can win, Prayer from out the lips of sin." What does it mean?

Virginia enters the Ghost's chamber. She is caught by the golden/yellow light in the room

The Ghost is taken by surprise and, thinking it to be a further attack by the Twins, dives for cover

Virginia It's OK, don't be frightened. It's me, it's Virginia.
Ghost Go away.
Virginia I've come to see if you're all right.
Ghost *(emerging)* I'm glorious, thank you. Now go away!
Virginia Oh, fine. If that's your attitude!
Ghost *(suddenly noticing Virgina's golden hair)* Wait! Don't move! Your hair in the light, it's — it's golden ... *(He looks up at the words on the stained glass window)* "When a golden girl can win."
Virginia *(looking up)* What a cool window!

Ghost (*rejecting the thought*) No — it can never be an American! (*He sits back on his throne*) I take it that you are not in the slightest bit frightened of me either.

Virginia Sorry.

Ghost A family trait, it seems. Your family quite clearly operates on a low, material plane of existence and are quite incapable of appreciating the symbolic value of sensuous phenomena. They are all horrid, rude, vulgar and dishonest.

Virginia You're being unfair.

Ghost Oh, am I!?

Virginia You've been "dishonest" too.

Ghost I most certainly have not!

Virginia You have. You've been stealing all the colours in my paint box and using them to replace that stain in the drawing-room. First all my red went, then the orange, and now I'm running short of blue. It's getting very silly. Anyway, blue is a ridiculous colour for blood.

Ghost Not at all. There's a great deal of blue blood in England.

Virginia The point is; you were being dishonest as well — you were stealing. And left me to paint the orchard in purple. And all the time, you were trying to make us think the stain was blood.

Ghost Well, what was I supposed to do? It's a very difficult thing to get real blood nowadays. And as your father began the whole thing with his range of modern bleaches, I saw no reason why I should not have your paints!

Virginia Look, I didn't come here to argue! I came to apologize. I came to — to check you were OK.

Ghost And what concern is that of yours?

Virginia I just thought — I was just worried for you.

Ghost Well, don't be. Now if you will forgive me, I have scheduled the next hundred years for a good sulk. The door is the wooden thing in the wall.

The Ghost turns away and ignores her. Virginia wanders around the chamber. She examines the various costumes around the chamber walls, and tries to make conversation

Virginia This costume looks great. I bet you really scared people with this.

Ghost (*looking round*) Yes, I did, as a matter of fact.

Virginia What character is it?

Ghost If you must know, that is my legendary persona as Gaunt Gideon, the blood-sucker of Bexley Moor. Armed with a rusty dagger, I would appear at midnight, gibber uncontrollably at the foot of a bed, then stab myself three times in the throat to the sound of Handel's *Water Music*.

Virginia Sounds great. (*Finding another costume*) And this one? Some sort of corpse?

Ghost The costume is incomplete, it requires a considerable "make-up", if you'll permit the theatrical terminology.

Virginia Sure.

Ghost I present it with white bleached bones and one rolling eyeball, and it has proved over the centuries to be quite as famous a role as those of Reckless Rupert and even Martin the Maniac.

Virginia What did you do that for?

Ghost Placing clammy hands on unsuspecting foreheads and hissing into trembling ears the awful secrets of the charnel house. It has excited quite a furore on summer evenings, particularly after a session of playing nine-pins with my bones on the tennis lawn.

Virginia laughs

And I even once played cards with Colonel Carbury who was to be found the next morning lying on the floor of the card-room in a helpless paralytic state, only able to utter the phrase "Double Sixes".

Virginia laughs again. But the mood of the Ghost suddenly darkens

But such delights are over now. Those days are over. The lights are dimmed. And I must remain in solitude.

Virginia I don't see why you have to.

Ghost Don't you? After these few weeks, it will never be the same again. The world is changing, it seems, and I no longer fill all hearts with dread. I have grown out of fashion. I have had my first taste of failure. And I see now the truth of it all. That this was all a game to me, a mask to hide behind. A shield from the reality of my lonely, miserable existence.

Virginia But can't someone help you? Help you get away from all this?

Ghost No. I am condemned to stay here forever.

Virginia Why? Is there a curse or something?

Ghost A curse that will never be broken.

Virginia How do you know? Have you ever tried?

Ghost Please. Please! Leave me to my misery. Go away!

Virginia Only if you tell me about the curse.

Ghost My dear girl, I am not in the habit of imparting ancient curses idly to strangers.

Virginia But I'm not a stranger. I'm someone who wants to help.

Ghost I am beyond help.

Virginia Won't you just explain the curse to me? All this mystery can get really irritating. Was it something to do with you murdering your wife? Mrs Umney told us you did.

Ghost That is a purely family matter and concerns no one else.

Virginia It concerns a lot of people. It's very bad to kill anyone!

Ghost Oh, you're so strict! I hate the cheap severity of abstract ethics! My wife was very plain, never had my ruffs properly starched and knew nothing about cookery!

Virginia You murdered her because she couldn't cook?

Ghost Oh, of course not!

Virginia Why then? (*Pause*) Why?

Ghost (*with a deep breath*) In truth; I hadn't meant to kill her at all. I did not hate her. I loved her. But I was insanely jealous. I thought her heart was leading her to other men, that she would one day leave me. And so we rowed and argued constantly. Then on a dark night one winter, in the middle of a terrible fight, I struck her — and she fell down the stairway — to her death. Poor, dear Eleanor, who had done nothing wrong. Dear old Ellie … Her brothers, intent on revenge, had me murdered and placed a curse on me — a curse that condemned me to remain as a spirit in this house.

Virginia How did they murder you?

Ghost They starved me to death.

Virginia Really? Gee — are you hungry? I could get you a sandwich.

Ghost You are very kind, but I have no stomach for it.

Virginia I know what it's like feeling you are all alone. Even living people have that sometimes. It seems endless, doesn't it? Like you'll never ever feel part of anything. That you could stop existing and no-one would notice. Sometimes it can be nice to have a friend.

Ghost Generally speaking, ghosts do not have "friends".

Virginia Then you can be unique. And I can be a ghost's friend.

Ghost Am I understanding this correctly? You wish to be a friend of an insane heartless murderer who has hounded a thousand people to within an inch of their lives and gorged the world with blood and misery? How do you pick your enemies?

Virginia Mom has always said I was strange. I guess she's right. Please. Let's be friends. I'd really like that.

Ghost I do not appear to have a choice.

Virginia Great. Let's shake on it.

Virginia spits on her hand, then offers it out

Ghost Did you just spit on that?

Virginia Oh, sorry — it's what we do at school, kind of a custom.

Ghost Well, I can assure you that it is by no means all the rage over here! Kindly wipe it clean.

Virginia wipes her hand on her clothes. This done, they shake hands

Virginia There. Done. I can now come and visit you all the time.
Ghost But ——
Virginia We're friends now. That's what you're supposed to do. Why don't I come here again, tomorrow?
Ghost I'll have to check my diary. Thursdays are never good for me. I have a regular appointment with my embalmer.
Virginia That's an English joke, isn't it? The travel agent warned us about those.

The Ghost gives a weak smile

Goodbye till tomorrow then. (*She makes her way towards the exit; turning back at the doorway*) Will this take me back to the drawing-room?
Ghost Just follow the eerie labyrinth. And make certain nobody sees you emerging back into the house. It is a private tunnel!
Virginia I understand. Goodbye, Ghost.

Virginia turns to leave. The Ghost stops her

Ghost Wait! Wait ... Tell me — just one thing ... Why? Why do you have any care for me?
Virginia I don't know. (*She touches her heart*) Something in here I guess. Goodbye, Sir Simon.

Virginia exits

The golden Light of the stained glass window intensifies. The Ghost notices this and thinks for a moment

Ghost "When a golden girl can win, Prayer from out the lips of sin" ...is the prophecy working at last? (*He sings*)

No. 12 A Ray of Light

Could she be the one that I wait for?
Could this be the chance that I dreamed?
Is there some hope at last?
A chink of light
A turning page
A spot of sun
As I reach for an end to my plight.

Dare I look at her face?
Do I see what I long for?
And in the darkness may I take
A moment to
Believe I'll break
The chains that hold me fast
At last?

A ray of light
That's all I need
Just give me the hope
That still I dream for
To end my empty years
Draw a veil of tears
Across my life
This fearful curse
Is my world a spell
That I can never reverse?
Yet there's light
A spark of light
That shines a smile on me
And a chance to be free.

As though in the far distance, we hear Virginia singing the chorus of "Poor Ghost"

Virginia (*voice only*) Are you lonely, poor Ghost?
Are you sad?
Where are you hiding now?
Do you need me?
Are your dreams, poor Ghost
A world you can't allow?
Are you weeping, poor Ghost?
Dry your eyes
And find a path from hell
Can you hear me?
Hear my voice, poor Ghost?
Break your life from this spell ...

Ghost   A ray of light
That's all I need
Let dawn gently cast aside my sorrow
And help me see the end

Through my gentle friend
A breath of life
This fearful curse
She might break the spell
That I could never reverse
Here there's light
A spark of light
That shines a smile on me
It's my chance to be free...

Black-out

SCENE 2

The front lawn of Canterville Chase. A sunny afternoon

Lucretia is reading a letter. Hiram, wearing knee pads, is trying out a cricket bat. The Twins are reading American comics

Lucretia Hyacinth writes that there's a new range of shoes at Macy's. The weather's lovely. I must write back and tell her that even England has managed to drag up a spot of sunshine today. Only the second time in three weeks! She apologizes for not writing more, she has to go iron the flag.

Hiram (*indifferently*) Terrific.

Lucretia I'm getting homesick already. I need some Americana. It's no good. I won't last out the summer here.

Hiram How do you know? At least give it a few more weeks.

Lucretia Just a medium-sized mall would be enough to keep me going, but there's not even that. The village is a joke; three shops full of people gossiping and apologizing — you knock into them and *they* say sorry. The only restaurant serves chunks of fried potato wrapped in newspaper — What do they call 'em, kids?

Twins (*in mock English accents*)"Chips!"

Lucretia It's scary, don't you think, Hiram? Hiram! I'm talking to you!

Hiram I'm learning cricket! I'm trying to concentrate!

Lucretia And I'm trying to survive! How do you expect me to cope? It's so dull here. Look at all this grass. How much green do they think a person can take?

Mrs Umney enters with a silver tray filled with cucumber sandwiches

Mrs Umney Here we are, a spot of luncheon for you.

Junior holds up one of the small sandwiches

Junior What is this?

Mrs Umney It's a cucumber sandwich.

Junior Are we supposed to eat it or laugh at it?

Mrs Umney I believe it's more nutritious if one eats it. If one simply laughs, one is both hungry and ridiculous — which is no way to spend a lunchtime.

Washington Whoever heard of putting cucumber into sandwiches. What about hot dogs? Ain't you got any hot dogs?

Mrs Umney No, we "Ain't"! Mrs Otis — a cucumber sandwich? Or do you object to them as well?

Lucretia Cucumber sandwich? Not at all — bring me two, right away.

Mrs Umney brings Lucretia two sandwiches. Lucretia removes the slices of cucumber from between the bits of bread and puts one slice over each eye

Fabulous. Thank you. (*She lies down to catch the sun*)

Mrs Umney takes the bits of bread back to the tray and then offers a plate of sandwiches to Hiram

Hiram I'll pass, thanks. You'd better give them to Virginia. If you can find her!

Mrs Umney Certainly. Will that be all, sir?

Hiram I guess so. Er — do you play sport?

Mrs Umney Not any more, sir. Not at my age.

Junior Why? Do they make you retire at ninety?

Mrs Umney gives Junior a stern look

Mrs Umney I'll be inside.

Mrs Umney exits

Junior I'm so bored with this place. It's so dull! (*Shouting*) So quiet! Now that the Ghost is leaving us alone, there's nothing to do.

Washington We haven't seen him in weeks! Bashing Simon de Canterville to bits was the only thing worth doing.

There is thunder. The sky darkens. It begins to rain

Lucretia Oh, I don't believe it. It's raining again! Oh, Hiram, do something about it.

Hiram This climate is a disgrace. Any more rain and we'll be swimming everywhere.

Washington Jeez, Pa. Do we have to put up with this for much longer? We're bored — and we're wet! Any more of this and we'll start turning bad.

Junior Or mouldy.
Hiram Look, what more do you want from me? This is England! I'm doing
my best!
Lucretia No more apologies, Hiram! And no more excuses. The boys are
right — enough is enough. Everywhere you look, culture and history —
it's a nightmare. I miss home too much. I want baseball. I want Hershey's.
I want my analyst! Time out, that's it. We want out of here. (*She sings*)

No. 13 Going Back To America

I've made up my mind
I don't want to be here
I've had enough
I'm getting bored
I wish that I was back abroad
I've made up my mind
I'm longing for sunshine
Had enough
This country grates
I want to be back in the States
You have to admit that our time here is through
So it leaves only one thing for all of us to do.

We're getting out
We're going home
We're packing up, we're getting tired,
We're gonna leave, we're not inspired.
We're taking a plane, a plane to the land of the free
We'll go tomorrow you can take it from me
Giving in, giving up, going crazy, going soon,
Making tracks,
Going back,
To America.

Twins
We've made up our minds
We don't want to be here
We've had enough
We're getting bored
We wish that we were back abroad
We've made up our minds
There's no more to break here
Had enough
This country sucks

And that Ghost was such a putz
We've always had each of our orders approved
We insist to you parents, it's time that we moved.

Twins ⎫
Lucretia ⎭
We're getting out
We're going home
We're packing up, we're getting tired,
We're gonna leave, we're not inspired.
We'll take a plane to the land of the free
We'll go tomorrow you can take it from me
Giving in, giving up, going crazy, going soon,
Making tracks,
Going back,
To America.

Hiram
I guess that I don't have a choice to make
All this green grass is more than I can take.
Cricket is beyond me
And gardens stump me too
Mushy peas and Yorkshire Pudding ——
I mean, what's a Yank to do?
I've made up my mind
We're packing to leave,
I've had enough
Of English wit —
Don't know why they laugh at it.
I could lose my mind
If I don't escape here
Had my fill of bread and jam
So we'll pack our bags and scram
Get clear of the land where embarrassment grew
And return to a place where they never like to queue!

All (*patriotically*) America, America
Across the mighty sea
They don't have haunted mansions there
In a land that's truly free.

We're getting out
We're going home (we're going home)
We're packing up, we're getting tired,
We're gonna leave, we're not inspired.
We'll take a plane to the land of the free

We'll go tomorrow you can take it from me.
Giving in, giving up, going crazy, going soon,
Making tracks, making moves,
Making sense, making changes,
Going now, going fast,
Going through, going back,
Gonna pack...
For America!

Virginia enters

Lucretia Ah, good, you're here. Go and pack.
Virginia What?
Lucretia We're leaving.
Virginia But we can't — not now. We have to stay.
Junior Why? Big Mouth.
Washington Who cares what you think anyway?
Lucretia What's the matter, don't you miss home?
Virginia Home is where the heart is, Ma.
Lucretia Don't get cute on me, Virginia.
Hiram Come on, honey, what's the problem?
Lucretia The same as usual — always the opposite to everything we do.
    You've been acting odd for weeks now. Come to think of it, you've been
    odd since the day you were born. But let's not get into that one again.
Virginia Why are you always putting me down? What is so wrong with me?
Hiram Nothing's "wrong" with you, Virginia. We just have trouble working
    out what is going on in that head of yours. For an Otis you're just —
    unusual.
Virginia You mean "different".
Junior No, Virginia. The word was "unusual" — strange, bizarre.
Washington Not of this planet!
Virginia You're right. I really don't fit in here. But at least I'm not the only
    one.
Junior You're not? You mean there's more like you out there?
Washington The population of Mars.

The Twins laugh

Virginia You can laugh all you like. I'm gonna spend the rest of my time with
    someone who understands.
Lucretia Mrs Umney doesn't understand you, Virginia. She's not a
    psychiatrist, she's a dusting machine.
Virginia I'm not talking about her.

Hiram It's OK, sweetie.
Virginia No! No, it's not. It never is!

Virginia marches off

Lucretia Well — this holiday really is doing your daughter some good — she's getting more English by the minute! Oh well — come on, boys, let's pack!

Black-out

SCENE 3

The Ghost's chamber

The Ghost is clearing all his props and costumes into some dusty old trunks. The shelves of the chamber are already half bare

Virginia arrives in the chamber

Ghost You're a few minutes late. It gave me quite a fright.
Virginia Sorry.
Ghost No, not at all. It's just that each day this week you have been so punctual. If you are more than two minutes behind, I start to worry that we will not see each other, and I do immensely enjoy our afternoons together. I am today in the process of clearing away all my props and costumes. I shall not need them for the rest of the summer.
Virginia Don't be so sure. My family are leaving, right away. They're packing now.

The Ghost suddenly goes pale with shock and becomes unsteady on his feet. Virginia rushes to him

Are you OK? What is it?
Ghost You mustn't go. This cannot happen.
Virginia I don't want to go. But if Ma decides to ——
Ghost You don't understand. It's ... (*He glances over at the enscribed window*)

Virginia notices him

Virginia Why did you look at that?
Ghost What?

Virginia The window. The writing — what does it mean?
Ghost It means I've been wasting my time for four hundred years. (*Angrily*)
My one hope dashed to the ground! You damned prophecy. Damn you for
raising my hopes!

Virginia walks over to the window

Virginia (*reading the writing on the window*) "When a golden girl can win,
Prayer from out the lips of sin". I don't understand.
Ghost It is merely the first two lines of the prophecy. It continues; "When
the barren almond bears, And a child gives away her tears, When the ——
Virginia "When the edge of darkness bodes not ill, Then shall all the house
be still, And peace come to Canterville".
Ghost (*suddenly animated*) You know it? You know the prophecy? How?
Virginia I don't know, I — I've never heard it before, it's just ——
Ghost Magic. Magic.
Virginia Tell me what the poem means.
Ghost It means that to escape the curse, a young girl must weep for me for
my sins, because I have no tears. She must then walk with me into the
darkness. A darkness where she would hear and see terrible things.
Monstrous shapes, hideous voices. There, amidst the horror, she must pray
for me, for my soul. And then, if she has always been sweet and good and
gentle, the barren almond tree in the garden will blossom. It is then through
an ancient ceremony known only to the Umneys that this golden girl must
walk with me to the very edge of darkness, risking everything yet again.
If such a sacrifice was made for someone who had committed such
appalling deeds as I, then it might be that the Angel of Death will have
mercy upon me. And I would at last be free.
Virginia Free? Free to go where?
Ghost When Englishmen die, they go to heaven.
Virginia And when Americans die, where do they go?
Ghost Paris.
Virginia Why didn't you tell me about this prophecy before?
Ghost I thought it of no interest to you.
Virginia That's not true. You were frightened about telling me. You thought
I might be your golden girl.
Ghost (*with a smile*) Dear Virginia, you are quite the most intelligent and
intuitive of souls. I see now that nothing escapes you. In truth, my dear, I
dared hope that you might be the one to break the curse. But I realize now
that I cannot ask this of you and that I should never expect it of anyone.
Virginia Why not?
Ghost Because of the nature of modern people. There are so few happy
princes to be found in the world. And only a happy prince can help me.
Someone who gives of everything.

Virginia I don't understand what you mean by a "happy prince".
Ghost It's an old legend, a story.
Virginia I'd like to hear it — will tell it to me?
Ghost Very well.

No. 14 The Happy Prince

(*Speaking*) High above the city, on a tall column, stood the statue of a prince.

With a gesture, the Ghost conjures a puff of smoke

The figure of the Prince, played by one of the Phantom Chorus, is revealed in the smoke. The face of the Prince is solemn as he takes the stance of a statue. He is dressed in a long, golden coat

A cloudy blue sky is created in the background by lighting, projection effects or the revealing of a simple backdrop

He was gilded all over with leaves of fine gold. For eyes, he had two bright sapphires and he was admired far and wide, not least of all by the town councillors.

The Ghost takes a coloured handkerchief from his pocket, the colours of which resemble a swallow. He flaps the handkerchief in the air as if it were a bird in flight

One day, there flew over the city a little Swallow. Seeking rest, he nestled himself at the feet of the golden statue. (*He lays the handkerchief at the foot of the Prince*) But just as he was putting his head under his wing, a large drop of water fell on him. "How curious!" thought the Swallow, for there was not a single cloud in the sky and no sign at all of rain. The Swallow looked up and saw that the drop had come from the eyes of the statue; tears were running down his golden cheeks. "Why are you weeping?" asked the Swallow. And the Prince looked down at the little bird and replied ...

During the following, whenever the Ghost sings or speaks as the voice of the prince, the prince mouths the words in unison with the Ghost

(*Singing*)   From my place here in the sky
              I can see for miles around
              See the sadness and the poor here
              With their crying, hungry sound
              And I wish now I could change things

I could help all those I see
With my jewels here
In my eyes here
I could end some misery.

(*Speaking*) Far away, there is a little street and a poor house. One of the windows is open and through it I can see a woman. Her face is thin and worn. In a bed in the corner, her little boy is lying ill. He has a fever and he is crying. Swallow, little Swallow, my eyes are sapphires. Will you pluck one of them out and take it to the poor child?

The Swallow felt sorry for the Prince in his sadness and so —(*he takes up the handkerchief*) the Swallow plucked out the Sapphire. (*He reaches towards the Prince's eye and with a sleight of hand trick a sapphire appears in his hand. He nestles the sapphire into the handkerchief*)

From this moment on, the Prince keeps one eye firmly closed (or applies an eye patch to it)

And then the Swallow flew out across the city! (*Quickly palming (hiding) the sapphire in his hand, he throws the handkerchief into the air*)

Magically, the handkerchief takes flight. This is achieved by the handkerchief being attached to a thin wire. The handkerchief's journey through the air is operated from backstage by use of a fishing rod or similar device. In the event of this being technically too difficult, the handkerchief can be palmed and the Ghost and Virginia can follow the bird's imagined path across the sky

(*Singing*) The Swallow flew and cut the air
Saw the city far below
Through the night, taking flight
To the place the prince had asked of him to go

The mother, played by a member of the Phantom Chorus, enters. During the following, as the lyrics describe, she mimes finding the sapphire and showing her joy

The mother saw a sapphire bright
Shining upon a chair
Full of joy, her little boy
Would now be cured with a nurse's love and care
And all because
Of a statue of a prince.

The mother exits

The handkerchief returns to the Ghost's hand, or else it disappears from view and he produces a new one from his pocket

(*Speaking*) The next day, the Prince called again to the Swallow. "Dear Swallow, in the Square below, I see a little girl trying to sell matches. She has no shoes or stockings and her little head is bare. You must pluck out my other jewelled eye and take it to her." "I cannot do that," the Swallow replied. "It will make you quite blind." "Please do as I ask," said the Prince. And so the Swallow took the jewel of the Prince's eye and flew out across the city again. So from that day, a little matchgirl and her family could live their lives in comfort.

The Prince closes or covers over his other eye

> (*Singing*)   And all because
>   Of a statue of a prince.

(*Speaking*) Then the Swallow came back to the Prince. "You are blind now," he said. "So I will stay with you always." And the Swallow fell asleep at his feet. (*He lays the handkerchief at the feet of the Prince*) The next day and for many weeks to come, the Swallow would fly over the city and tell the statue of all the misery he saw there. "I am covered with fine gold," said the Prince. "You must take it off, leaf by leaf, and give it to the poor." So, the Swallow picked off the leaves of fine gold and took them out across the city as the Prince had requested.

Another member of the Phantom Chorus enters and removes the Prince's golden coat, revealing grey and dull garments beneath

And though the once golden statue now began to look dull and grey, he was at last happy with the work they had done.

> (*Singing*) From my place here in the sky
>   I have reached for miles around
>   No more sadness, no more poor here
>   With their crying hungry sounds
>   And I know now I have changed things
>   I have helped all those you see
>   With the gold here
>   That once shined here
>   I have ended misery.

(*Speaking*)"Oh, Swallow, are you not as content as I?" "I am indeed", said the Swallow, "but I am also very cold. For I did not migrate to warmer climes so that I could stay at your side. And I have been so very proud to be your friend." And with that, the Swallow fluttered down to the Prince's feet for the last time, and was no more. The Swallow had gone, the jewels had gone, and the gold had gone. The Mayor of the City and his town Councillors ——

Members of the Chorus enter and take the role of the Mayor and his Councillors. They stand dimly lit and in the distance, as though at the feet of the statue, they look upwards and seem appalled at the state of their once glorious statue

—— were appalled that such a shabby statue now stood above them. And so they ordered that the Statue be pulled down at once and melted in a furnace.

The Mayor and councillors exit

The blue sky fades out

The Prince slowly exits, but the handkerchief remains

But for all the heat in the fire, they could not melt the golden heart of the Prince. And to this day, if you were to ask any wise person what were the two most precious things to ever come out of that forsaken city — they will tell you of a faithful Swallow (*he picks up the handkerchief*) and a happy Prince.

The Phantom Chorus sing in gentle harmony off stage

Ghost }   Such precious things are rare indeed
Phantoms }   So think of the tale I sing
                        Be aware, you must care
                        For the riches that a deed of love can bring
                        And all because
                        Of a statue of a Prince
                        And all because…

Ghost (*speaking*) Of a faithful Swallow and a happy Prince.

All (*singing*)   With golden hearts…

At the end of the story, Virginia is deeply moved and is crying

Ghost Oh, my dear child, you're crying.

Virginia I'm sorry, I can't help it.

Ghost Do not apologize. To be sensitive is a great gift. It means you are in touch with your heart. I admire that quality enormously.

Virginia Is that the truth?

Ghost Of course, it's the truth. We don't tell lies in England, it is considered very bad manners. Here, wipe your eyes. (*He offers her a dusty handkerchief from his pocket*)

Virginia (*refusing the handkerchief*) It's OK, I've got my own. Yours has cobwebs on it.

Ghost Oh, yes. Sorry. (*He puts his dusty handkerchief away*)

Virginia I see now what you meant before. And I think that I could be a happy prince. I could help you. I'll do anything I can for you.

Ghost You are so sweet and kind —but, no. It is too great a risk, too dark and frightening. There you would see such terrible things that it would mean the loss of your innocence, the shattering of the precious gift of youth. And I would rather suffer here for centuries than see you terrified.

Virginia I don't frighten that easy.

Ghost Virginia ——

Virginia I don't have time to argue. I'll be OK. Just trust me.

Ghost Would you really do this for me? I had no idea you were quite so brave.

Virginia Neither did I.

Ghost My dear, dear child.

Virginia Where do we go?

Ghost Just take my hand.

They stand together before the window and hold hands. The Ghost raises his other hand into the air

Light shines through the stained glass window. There is a rumble. The glass cracks apart and the whole wall opens, revealing darkness beyond. There is the sound of an eerie wind and disturbing animalistic howling noises. The Ghost remains frozen at the entranceway. Virginia is first to step through. She reaches back for the Ghost's hand and leads him into the darkness. Thunder and lightning. The crack in the wall closes up behind them

The Lights fade to Black-out

SCENE 4

The drawing-room of Canterville Chase

Hiram is standing alone in the middle of the room

Hiram (*calling out*) Virginia! Virginia! Virginia, where are you?

Lucretia enters

Lucretia It's ridiculous, I can't find her anywhere.
Hiram We're not gonna make that flight.
Lucretia We better. She can't have gone far, we saw her just a few hours ago.

Mrs Umney enters, carrying a dusty leather-bound book

Hiram Mrs Umney, we can't find Virginia — she hasn't even packed her ——
Mrs Umney (*stopping Hiram*) It is all right, Mr Otis. She will be with us soon.
Hiram Well where ——
Mrs Umney All will be explained in good time. But for now, I need you to go into the garden and fetch the Twins here.
Hiram Now just a ——
Mrs Umney (*firmly*) Right away!
Hiram (*frightened*) Yes ma'am.

Hiram exits immediately

Mrs Umney Go with him, Mrs Otis, there is not a second to waste.
Lucretia I think you'd better ——
Mrs Umney Now! Mrs Otis!
Lucretia You're pushing your luck, Umney — I want answers when I get back.

Lucretia exits after Hiram

There is a loud rumble

After a moment, Virginia stumbles into the room from the opposite doorway. She looks exhausted and is covered in dust and cobwebs

Mrs Umney rushes to her

Mrs Umney My dear child. I have visited the chamber — I know the great deed which you have done. Are you all right?

Virginia Yes. Yes, I am. Where's the Ghost?

Mrs Umney He will be with us shortly. The end of his torment is at last in sight. But there is a final, ancient procedure that must be undertaken, a ceremony through which the spell can be broken. It must begin at the striking of the hour. You can leave this to me — the Umneys know what to do. (*She gestures to the book that she has with her*) We have always known what to do. Your family will be here soon and I must talk to them. We need their help, all of them.

Virginia But what if they don't want to help? They can be very difficult.

Mrs Umney They have to be persuaded. It's a matter of life or death! They absolutely *must* be persuaded to assist us.

Virginia My family? They never will.

Mrs Umney That is my fear. But I must try.

Virginia It's OK — leave it to me.

Mrs Umney But ——

Virginia They have to start listening to me at some point. Today's a good time to start.

Mrs Umney If you're sure?

Virginia nods that she is

I must get everything prepared. Bless you for helping the Ghost.

Mrs Umney exits as Hiram, Lucretia, Junior and Washington enter

Lucretia There she is! Where have you been?

Virginia Ma, there isn't time to explain in full, but I need your help.

Lucretia What? Do you need money?

Virginia No, Ma. Have you just been in the garden?

Junior What about it?

Virginia That dead tree in the middle, were there white flowers?

Washington Yeah, yeah there were. How did you know?

Virginia (*smiling*) You see — that's part of the prophecy; "When the barren almond bears…"

Lucretia Really, darling? That's nice. (*Aside to Hiram*) Quick, get a doctor.

Virginia I need you all to listen, very carefully. You have to help me — well, not me; the Ghost.

Hiram The Ghost? What are you talking about?

Virginia The Ghost has been under a spell. A curse that is nearly broken. And all that we have to do now is an ancient ceremony and he can be free, forever.

Lucretia Ceremony?
Virginia That's right, Ma — and it requires a lot of people to take part. I need you to help us.
Hiram Honey, I think you just need some rest.
Lucretia You're delusional, sweetie.
Virginia I am not! Just because you don't understand what's going on here, you decide to dismiss it. But I won't let you. For once you have to just listen to me. We have to help the Ghost.
Hiram Virginia, what has been going on here? Have you been meeting with this Ghost?
Virginia Every day. We've become great friends.
Lucretia Terrific. The first friend she's had in years — and it's a dead guy!
Virginia There's more to him than that. The Ghost is special. He has shown me what life is, and what death is… and why love is stronger than both …(*She sings*)

No. 15 Taking a Stand

I know that you think that I'm weak at heart
I know that you feel that we're worlds apart
But we have the chance to start again
A chance to help a friend.
Join me, please.
I can't do this without you.
Join me, please,
Help me save the man.
Please. Please.

All (*except Virginia, speaking*) No!

Virginia (*singing*) Then I'll stand here until I persuade you to.
I will not be delayed by resistance from you.
I'm standing my ground
Until I've found
That you will lend a hand.
Virginia, Virginia,
Is taking a stand.

Taking a stand
I'm taking a stand
Take the bull by the horns
And the route is planned
Find the strength to persist

I am in command
The spell can be broken
Freedom can be born
Virginia has spoken
I'm taking a stand.

I know you believe that it's time to run
I know that you feel that your plans are done
But I'm sure in my heart of the task ahead
Don't you hear a word I've said?
Join me, please
I can't do this without you
Join me, please
Help me save the man.
Please.
Please.

*Everyone looks away from Virginia, except for Lucretia. Virginia approaches
her mother*

The music continues to underscore

Virginia Ma?
Lucretia Listen to this, Hiram. Our daughter is finally getting passionate
about something! This is what I've been waiting for! She's gonna be just
like her mother!
Hiram God help us...

Lucretia (*singing*)Virginia, Virginia,
                        Is taking a stand!

Virginia ⎫   Taking a stand
Lucretia ⎭   We're taking a stand
                    Take the bull by the horns
                    And the route is planned
                    Find the strength to persist
                    We are in command
                    The spell can be broken
                    Freedom can be born
                    Virginia has spoken
                    We're taking a stand.

> Join us, please,
> We can't do this without you.
> Join us please, help us save the man.
> Please. Please…

Hiram (*speaking*) Oh, I don't know — what do you say, boys?

The Twins shrug, clearly not yet persuaded

Mrs Umney enters, carrying two plates of hot dogs

Mrs Umney What do you say, boys?

Junior's and Washington's eyes light up

Twins Hot dogs!

They grab a hot dog each and hold them triumphantly into the air

All (*Singing*) Taking a stand! We're taking a stand!
Taking a stand
We're taking a stand
Take the bull by the horns
And the route is planned
Find the strength to persist
We are in command
The spell can be broken
Freedom can be born
Virginia has spoken
Virginia has spoken
We're — taking — a stand…

During the audience applause, Mrs Umney whispers into Virginia's ear

Virginia rushes off

Mrs Umney Please sit down at once. I have the details of the ceremony here.
(*She opens the large leather-bound volume and blows the dust from it*)

A huge cloud of dust billows forward. Everyone coughs

Sorry. (*Reading*) "The Ghost must walk with his ancient bride
                    Where angelic brothers stand on either side
                    And look to be blessed by a beggar's hand
                    If the prophecy was broken by an honest pledge
                    Then the Ghost may walk to the darkness' edge."
Lucretia I don't get it.
Washington It's stupid!
Junior It doesn't make sense!
Mrs Umney Oh, but it does. It merely dictates that certain characters must
assemble. You see — Virginia must be the bride with true love for the
Ghost. (*To Lucretia and Hiram*) There must be beggars and — (*a strained
look*) — angelic brothers!
Twins Us?!
Mrs Umney (*with a sigh*) Yes…! Will you do this for your sister? She has
been very brave.
Junior Virginia? Brave?
Mrs Umney Oh yes, braver and stronger than any of us ever imagined.
Washington I didn't know she had it in her.
Mrs Umney Perhaps such bravery runs in the family?
Junior It does!
Mrs Umney Then I know you will have no second thoughts about taking
your role … And there may be another hot dog in it for you.

The Twins nod excitedly

Good. Wait for me in the corridor.

The Twins run off

And Mrs Otis, we must get you into your costume.
Lucretia Yes, now about that — I'm playing a beggar!?
Mrs Umney No time to dally, Mrs Otis.

Mrs Umney rushes Hiram and Lucretia off

Black-out

SCENE 5

The drawing-room of Canterville Chase

A clock chimes the hour. The chimes echo loudly

The Lights come up on a different portrait of Simon de Canterville. There are now two figures in the portrait: Simon and his wife Eleanor. Eleanor bears a striking resemblance to Virginia (Note: the change of portrait is not essential)

Mrs Umney enters with the book. A spotlight comes up on her

No. 16 The Spell

Phantoms (*off; singing*) Ah (*etc.*)

Mrs Umney   The Ghost must walk with his ancient bride
                        Where angelic brothers stand on either side
                        And look to be blessed by a beggar's hand
                        And if the spirits wish it too
                        He may then take his stand
Phantoms (*off*)   Ah (*etc.*)
                        Ah (*etc.*)
Mrs Umney   If the prophecy was broken by an honest pledge
                        Then the Ghost may walk to the darkness' edge.

The Lights come up on the room

Lucretia and Hiram enter dressed as sixteenth-century beggars

Mrs Umney Mrs Otis, you look wonder ——
Lucretia I'd rather not talk about it!
Hiram OK, Umney, so where are the boys?

Mrs Umney gestures to the doorway

The Twins enter. They are both dressed like angels, in white smocks and with golden halos fixed above their heads. They look totally disgruntled

Mrs Umney stands the Twins in position. Distant thunder

The Phantom Chorus, offstage, sing open vowel sounds ("oohs" and "ahs" etc.) to tune of song No. 16 The Spell

The lighting changes

Slowly and one by one, members of the Phantom Chorus enter from the edges of the stage. Each is dressed in white or grey. They gather in far corners of the set, as though witnesses to the ceremony about to begin. Hiram and Lucretia are slightly disturbed by the presence of so many mysterious figures, but the Twins just continue to look disgruntled. When everyone is in position, Mrs Umney proceeds

Mrs Umney It is time...

Virginia and the Ghost walk into the room. Virginia is dressed in an elaborate sixteenth-century bridal outfit

Lucretia Oh — my — God!

The Ghost shakes the hand of each beggar and acknowledges the Twins. Then, taking Virginia's hand, they wait in position at the front of the stage. Suddenly, amid a great rumbling and cracking noise, the huge portrait of Sir Simon de Canterville opens outwards revealing a dark area beyond, shrouded in ghostly fog

Mrs Umney (*to the Ghost*) You must go.

The remainder of the Phantom Chorus enter, bringing on a set of steps. They place them leading up to the area of the open portrait

A rumble on the piano (perhaps with other instruments) provides an improvised under-scoring for the next few moments

The Ghost begins to walk slowly up the stairway, Virginia watching him intently. As he reaches the top, Virginia rushes up the stairway to join him

Virginia, no!
Hiram What's going on?
Mrs Umney You must call her back. If she goes with him, she is lost to you forever.
Hiram (*yelling*) Virginia, honey, what are you doing?
Virginia I want to be with him — I want to be with my friend.
Lucretia No! You belong here with us — with your family!
Virginia I can't leave him. (*She takes a step closer*)
Junior Virginia, don't!
Washington Come back, sis!

Virginia takes the Ghost's hand. Lucretia runs to the base of the steps

Lucretia Virginia! We love you!

There is a loud crack of thunder. The Ghost falls to his knees. Virginia rushes down the stairway and into her mother's arms. The family all gather round her. The Ghost looks into the sky

Ghost Eleanor? Dearest wife? Forgive me for my grievous sin. Let the heart of this golden child and the love of her family release me from this torment. Give me your blessing. I beg you.

The voice of Eleanor is heard

Eleanor's Voice I forgive you ... I had always forgiven you. All you needed to do — was show love.

Music underscoring "A Ray of Light" begins

The Phantom Chorus drift off

Suddenly, beyond the portrait, there is a blinding golden light which pierces the darkness. The Ghost looks up in wonder. He stands, full of joy

Mrs Umney Go now, Sir Simon. You are free!

The Ghost walks into the light — and disappears beyond the portrait

The music crescendos

The portrait closes and the Lights return to normal

Hiram Gee — that was quite something. How the hell do we follow that?
Lucretia Well, maybe we should stage — (*she looks at the Twins*) — a Nativity play!

Lucretia and Hiram laugh

Junior Oh, very funny, Ma!
Washington Yeah, you're a real riot!
Virginia The whole house suddenly seems so different, doesn't it.
Hiram It sure does.
Lucretia You know what, Hiram ——

Music underscoring "Poor Ghost" begins

— I think Canterville Chase might just grow on us. Why don't we stay a few more weeks?

Hiram Whatever you want, Lucretia, whatever you want.

Hiram and Lucretia embrace. Virginia is thrilled and hugs Mrs Umney

Mrs Umney Well, — I think I'd better go and make us all a nice cup of tea.

Mrs Umney heads off. Junior and Washington spit on their hands and offer them to Virginia. Delighted, she shakes their hands. Hiram and Lucretia watch this happily, their arms around each other

A crescendo of music and the Lights fade to Black-out

The cast take individual bows. Once all the cast and chorus are on stage they sing

No. 17 The Tale Of The Canterville Ghost (Finale)

All
> You sat back and stared
> At the spirit that we shared
> You let us be your host
> For the tale, for the tale, for the tale, for the tale
> For (the Canterville) the tale, for the tale, for the tale
> Of the Canterville... Of the Canterville
> — Ghost!

CURTAIN

FURNITURE AND PROPERTY LIST

ACT I
PRELUDE

Pre-set: Interior of Canterville Chase drawing-room:
Armchairs
Table and chairs
Cobwebs
Antique electrical lamps
Grandfather clock
Mantelpiece. *On it*: various ornaments
Shelves of books
Umbrella stand. *In it*: umbrellas
Large tudor-style portrait of Simon de Canterville
Oriental-looking curtains over the window

SCENE 1

Set: Sign reading "Canterville Station"

Off stage: Luggage containing umbrella (**Hiram**)
Luggage containing umbrella and night case (**Lucretia**)
Luggage containing umbrella (**Virginia**)
Luggage containing umbrella (**Washington**)
Luggage containing umbrella and torch (**Junior**)

During black-out on page 5

Strike: Sign

Off stage: Night case with trick wire attached (**Lucretia**)

Personal: **Hiram**: bottle of "Otis's Champion Stain Remover", rag
Twins: filled water pistols

SCENE 2

On stage: Four-poster bed.
Bedside table. *On it*: small bottle of "Otis's Rising Sun Lubricator"
American magazine for **Lucretia**

Off stage: Pillows (**Twins**)

Personal: **Ghost**: cobwebs, heavy manacles, rusty chains

Scene 3

On stage: Stained glass window
                The **Ghost**'s costumes. *On them*: thick dust, cobwebs
                Props. *On them*: thick dust, cobwebs
                Chests. *On them*: thick dust, cobwebs
                Shelves. *On them*: busts and skulls
                Portraits
                Mirror
                Battered sixteenth-century throne

Scene 4

On stage: Interior for drawing-room as Scene 1
                Table and chairs
                Chair for **Virginia**
                Tea-trolley. *On it*: bowls, jugs of water, teacups, a tureen of porridge,
                    a pot of tea and a milk jug

Off stage: 3 enormous cigars (**Hiram, Twins**)
                Plate of biscuits (**Mrs Umney**)
                Large axe (**Ghost**)
                Large white sheet and scythe (**Twins**)

Personal: **Ghost:** fake hand

Scene 5

On stage: Interior for drawing-room as Scene 1
                Elaborate traps looking like an army assault course. Including a
                    tripping rope, some buckets of water
                New York newspaper for **Hiram**

Off stage: A white handkerchief, small British flag, American flag (**Ghost**)

Personal: **Ghost:** a papier mâché head or a football head

ACT II
SCENE 1

On stage: Interior of **Ghost**'s chamber as ACT 1, SCENE 3
Large leather-bound book set behind throne

SCENE 2

On stage: Letter for **Lucretia**
Cricket bat for **Hiram**
American comics for the **Twins**

Off stage: A silver tray filled with cucumber sandwiches (**Mrs Umney**)

Personal: **Hiram**: cricket knee pads

SCENE 3

On stage: Interior of **Ghost**'s chamber
Shelves half bare
Dusty trunks. *In them*: some of the props and costumes
Cloud backdrop (optional)

Personal: **Ghost**: trick swallow-coloured handkerchief attached to wire (1 extra
    swallow-coloured handkerchief if required), sapphire, dusty
    handkerchief
Prince: 2 eye-patches (if required)

SCENE 4

On stage: Interior for drawing-room

Off stage: Dusty leather-bound book (**Mrs Umney**)
Two plates of hot dogs (**Mrs Umney**)

Personal: **Virginia**: dust and cobwebs

SCENE 5

On stage: Interior for drawing-room
Different portrait of Simon de Canterville with his wife Eleanor
    (Optional)

Off stage: Set of steps (**Members of the Chorus**)

LIGHTING PLOT

Practical fittings required: nil

Interiors. The drawing-room of Canterville Chase, The Ghost's chamber, Hiram's and Lucretia's bedroom. Exteriors. The lawn of Canterville Chase

ACT I, PRELUDE

To open: Dim light

Cue 1	The **Chorus** strikes a group pose *Black-out*	(Page 2)

ACT I, SCENE 1

To open: Black-out

Cue 2	Sound of a train pulling away from station. When ready *Lights rise on Canterville station platform*	(Page 3)
Cue 3	**Mrs Umney**: (*singing*) "Welcome to your home." *Rain effect*	(Page 4)
Cue 4	Roll of thunder *Flash of lightning, then black-out. When ready bring up full interior lighting*	(Page 5)
Cue 5	At the end of the song *Bring up red spotlight in corner of room*	(Page 7)
Cue 6	The **Twins** proceed to rub the stain *Slowly fade red spotlight*	(Page 9)
Cue 7	Rumble of thunder *Flash of lightning*	(Page 10)
Cue 8	More thunder *Flashes of lightning light the face on the portrait*	(Page 10)
Cue 9	More loud thunder *Flashes of lightning very bright. Sudden black-out*	(Page 10)

ACT 1, SCENE 2

To open: General interior lighting

ACT 1, Scene 3

To open: General interior lighting

Cue 23	Thunder *Flashes of lightning, black-out*	(Page 22)

ACT 1, Scene 4

To open: Morning. General interior lighting

Cue 24	At the end of the Song No. 7 An American Abroad *Create stain with yellow spot in corner of room*	(Page 28)
Cue 25	Thunder *Flashes of lightning*	(Page 31)
Cue 26	**Virginia** stares at the portrait *Close lights in on* **Virginia** *and the portrait*	(Page 34)
Cue 27	At the end of the song *Fade to black-out*	(Page 36)

ACT I, Scene 5

To open: Evening. General interior lighting. Blue spotlight stain in corner of room

Cue 28	Thunder *Flashes of lightning. Then flash of green smoke*	(Page 37)
Cue 29	**Virginia** walks forward and stops for a moment *Lighting change*	(Page 39)
Cue 30	**Virginia** exits *Fade to black-out*	(Page 39)

ACT II, Scene 1

To open: Dim lighting

Cue 31	The **Chorus** exits *Lighting change. Golden light through stained glass window*	(Page 41)
Cue 32	**Virginia** exits *Increase golden light through window*	(Page 45)

ACT II, Scene 5

To open: Darkness

Cue 44	A clock chimes the hour *Bring up spot on the portrait*	(Page 65)
Cue 45	**Mrs Umney** enters *Bring up spotlight on **Mrs Umney***	(Page 65)
Cue 46	**Mrs Umney**: " ... to the darkness' edge." *Bring up general interior lighting*	(Page 65)
Cue 47	The **Chorus** sing open vowel sounds off stage *Lighting change*	(Page 65)
Cue 48	The portrait cracks open *Change lighting to ghostly darkness beyond the portrait*	(Page 66)
Cue 49	The **Chorus** drift off *Blinding golden light piercing the darkness beyond the portrait*	(Page 67)
Cue 50	The portrait closes *Revert to general interior lighting*	(Page 67)
Cue 51	A crescendo of music *Fade to black-out*	(Page 68)
Cue 52	When ready *Bring up lighting for finale*	(Page 68)

EFFECTS PLOT

ACT I

Cue 13   Ghoulish geen light pierces through the frame of the door   (Page 16)
Opening door creak. Swirling mist through open door.
Eerie music, rolls of thunder and distant blood-curdling screams

Cue 14   The **Ghost** waves his guts   (Page 17)
Lots of revolting noises

Cue 15   The **Ghost** tosses the bottle to the floor   (Page 18)
Almighty moan

Cue 16   The lights fade to black-out   (Page 18)
Sound of the family's laughter echoes loudly and continually
   through the scene change

Cue 17   The **Chorus** form a final triumphant pose   (Page 22)
Thunder

Cue 18   The **Ghost** enters   (Page 29)
Loud crash of thunder

Cue 19   The **Ghost** trips and exits   (Page 29)
Medley of tumbling thumps, crashes and screams

Cue 20   The **Ghost** wrenches off his hand   (Page 31)
Revolting sound effect

Cue 21   The **Ghost**: " ... over yet!"   (Page 31)
Thunder

Cue 22   **Washington**: "Thanks, Ma."   (Page 36)
Roll of thunder in the near distance

Cue 23   **Junior**: " ... it's too dangerous."   (Page 37)
The distant sounds of ghostly moaning and rattling his chains

Cue 24   The **Twins** get ready with their traps   (Page 37)
Ghost's *moaning gets louder. Thunder*

Cue 25   Lightning flashes   (Page 37)
Flash of green smoke

Cue 26   The **Ghost** parades about the room   (Page 38)
Resounding echo effect on **Ghost**'s *voice, dialogue pp 37/38*

Cue 27   **Ghost**: " Behold the thunder!"   (Page 37)
Thunder

Cue 28	**Ghost**: " Behold the screams!" *Sounds of screams*	(Page 37)

ACT II

Cue 29	**Washington**: " ... worth doing." *Thunder*	(Page 48)
Cue 30	The sky darkens *Sound of rain*	(Page 48)
Cue 31	The **Ghost** makes a gesture *A puff of smoke*	(Page 54)
Cue 32	Light shines through the stained glass window *A rumble*	(Page 58)
Cue 33	The window cracks open *Eerie wind and disturbing animalistic howling noises*	(Page 58)
Cue 34	**Virginia** leads the **Ghost** into the darkness *Thunder*	(Page 58)
Cue 35	**Lucretia** exits *Loud rumble*	(Page 59)
Cue 36	To open SCENE 5 *Clock chimes the hour, loudly with echo effect*	(Page 65)
Cue 37	**Mrs Umney** stands the **Twins** in position *Distant thunder*	(Page 65)
Cue 38	As the portrait opens *Rumbling and cracking noises. Ghostly fog*	(Page 66)
Cue 39	**Lucretia**: " We love you!" *Loud crack of thunder*	(Page 67)
Cue 40	**Ghost**: " I beg you." *Voice of **Eleanor** as dialogue page 67*	(Page 67)

Lightning Source UK Ltd.
Milton Keynes UK
UKHW021821230519
343218UK00008B/696/P